Mother Shirley

No Cost Too Great in Following Jesus

Part of the Focused Lives Series

Becky Durben

ISBN 978-1-932814-01-9

The cover pencil sketching of Shirley Raper was drawn by Melissa Williams.

This e-book is available from:
Barnabas Publishers
2175 North Holliston Avenue
Altadena, CA 91001

Table of Contents

Preface

Last year, God catapulted an obscure verse to prominence in my life because of a class I took at Fuller Seminary. The class was Focused Lives, designed by Dr. Robert J. Clinton, and taught by Wilmer Villacorta. It is a verse that is and will forever refine my focus as I press on to finish my life well. It is:

> Remember your former leaders. Think back on how they lived and ministered. Imitate those excellent qualities you see in their lives, for Jesus Christ is the same today as he was in the past and as He will be in the future. What He did for them He will do for you to inspire and enable your leadership.
>
> Hebrews 13:7, 8 (J. R. Clinton's Interpretive Paraphrase)

Eight years prior to taking the Focused Lives class, I met Mother Shirley. She was the embodiment of Christ's love. At the time, she was in her sixties. Some friends invited me to attend the spiritual retreat she planned that fall. I am not a crier, yet every time I walked into the room where the gathering took place, once the session started, I wept uncontrollably. A profound healing took place within my spirit that weekend.

People love to sit and listen to Mother Shirley. It does not matter if it is in a bible study setting, having a morning chat, praying with her, or as a passenger in her car on the way to town. She speaks the wisdom of God, learned through years of making godly choices, often in the face of adversity.

In 2005, I asked Mother Shirley if anyone was writing her life story, as I wanted to write her story. She said no. Shocked, I offered to write her biography. I was thrilled when she said that she would be honored if I wrote her story.

The following spring, in May 2006, I was a Teacher's Assistant for Dr. Clinton, for his Mentoring class. I approached him and told him that I wanted to write the biography of this wonderful woman, who I looked to as a mentor. I asked him for some guidance and suggestions. He recommended that I write her biography using the Focused Lives format. He explained that he was looking for good biographies of Christian women who had finished their lives well. Excited and honored that Dr. Clinton said that he would publish this biography for use in his class, I asked Mother Shirley if I could spend a week with her to pursue this dream of mine. In June of 2006, my daughter-in-love, Katie and I flew to Tennessee, to spend one week with her for the interview.

In the summer of 2007, I enrolled in the Focused Lives class. Until then, I felt frustrated that I had not started writing her biography. Now, I realize the timing was wrong. I needed to take the class prior to writing her Focused Life biography. Here it is, June, 2008 and the biography is finished in God's time and not mine. It is a gift of love to a woman who decided when she accepted the Lord, that no cost would be too great in following Him. May your life be changed as a result of reading her story!

Shirley Raper's biography is organized using the Focused Lives format, Dr. Clinton developed. This format enables the student, to examine the paradigms and life situations that shaped and molded the leader. It is like a road map that enables the reader to see what the leader did, and how the leader did it to arrive at the "finished well" destination.

Some points of clarification include all book titles mentioned in this biography are emboldened. The page numbering for Dr. Clinton's **Mentoring Handbook** is unique. The page number is labeled according to the chapter number and the page number within the chapter. For example, page 15 in chapter 2 is labeled 2-15. It should be noted that the term PHASE is always capitalized when used in a Focused Life biography as a matter of convention. The chapter designation in the biography portion is divided according to the PHASES of Mother Shirley's timeline.

Mother Shirley's biography begins after the introduction with two opening illustrations of incidences that shaped how she developed into a leader. These two opening illustrations are followed by her biography. There are five biographical chapters, called PHASES. The first PHASE is entitled, Emotional Orphan. The second PHASE is titled, Adopted by God, followed by Nurtured by God, transitioning into PHASE IV, Mother to All, and last, No Cost to Great.

Following the biographical section, the biography next examines critical incidences in Shirley's life. The goal is to discover patterns of development to enable the reader to see how the leader learned leadership skills, character, and destiny direction through events. Every leader's life is guided by a value system. Next, Shirley's values are written with a descriptor paragraph explaining how that value shapes her actions.

The next section deals with ministry insights gleaned from her life. Following that the biography examines those aspects that define a Focused Life biography: her unique methodologies, meaning her unique ways of doing ministry; quotes; ministry insights into her sphere of influence; her ultimate contribution set, labels describing her particular leadership calling; giftedness development, including natural, acquired, and spiritual; destiny processing; identification of major values that drove her life; ministry philosophy concepts, and paradigm shifts that helped to focus her life.

The following section, Overview of a Focused Life deals with her life purpose, her major role as a leader, followed by detailing her effective methodologies that set her apart as a leader, and her ultimate contribution. The conclusion contains suggestions for further study and an address should the reader want to contact Mother Shirley.

There are six appendices. They include her timeline so that the reader can follow the development of her life, a glossary, focal findings of her life, a section called Finishing Well Characteristics, her destiny log and last and most important, her personal life mandate.

Mother Shirley's life is worth studying. Her life is worth emulating. She is a Hebrews 13:7-8, leader!

Mother Shirley's life in pictures!
Shirley Ann Raper, because she was willing to pay the cost in knowing Jesus, she went from being an emotional orphan who longed to be loved to a spiritual mother who delights in loving all! Here is her life in pictures.

Shirley Ann 3 years old

Shirley Ann 12 years old

Mother Shirley and Pops!

That was then - 1957

This is now - 2006!

Above: Mar Michael, a Bishop in the Syrian Orthodox Church, Mother Shirley, and Jackie, a life-long friend. Left side: The chapel built next to her home. Below: Mother Shirley is leading church.

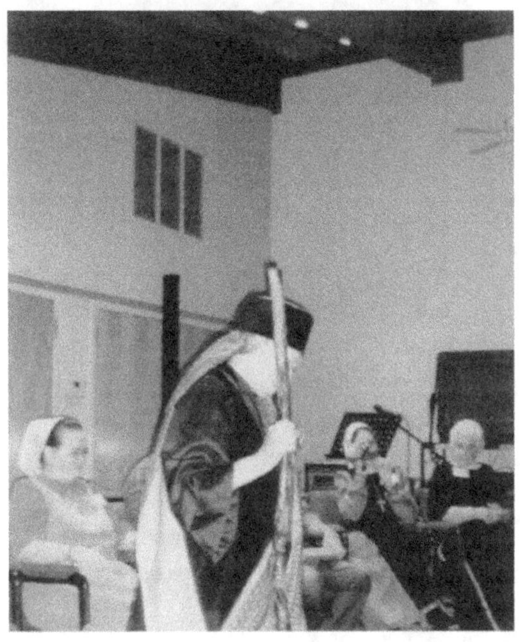

One of Mother Shirley's spiritual retreats celebrating the splendor of God's Presence! Mother Shirley is in the top two pictures. One of the dancers honoring God through celebratory dance and devotion!

Above: Libby dancing before the Lord. Below: Friday night dinner celebration.

INTRODUCTION

(Mother) Shirley Raper
(1933-)

> Remember your former leaders. Think back on how they lived and ministered. Imitate those excellent qualities you see in their lives, for Jesus Christ is the same today, as he was in the past and as He will be in the future. What He did for them He will do for you to inspire and enable your leadership.
> Hebrews 13:7, 8 (J. R. Clinton's Interpretive Paraphrase)

Let's remember Shirley Raper, a mother to the motherless, the broken and the marginalized She is a teacher extraordinaire exhaling the manifest and unbiased love of Christ to all within her sphere of influence from prison inmates to military generals. Her ability to extend intentional honor to all, be it in formal settings or informal, sets her apart as a leader who knows how to apply biblical truths to the prevailing culture redeeming that culture within her sphere of influence.

Let's remember Shirley Raper, a leader called by God to leadership roles that man not God, made gender specific. Her obedience to God trumped the culture pitting her against man-made systems at great personal cost to her. Here is a woman who decided when she accepted the Lord that no cost would be too great for her in following Jesus making her a rare leader God could trust.

Opening Illustration I:

"His Eye is on the Sparrow"
Radical Committal Foundation Pattern[1]
Age: 33

Faithfulness was a quality missing from Shirley's life growing up. Her parents divorced in 1940 at a time when divorce was rare and considered a stigma. Her father owned a bar and as a small child she loved to spend time there with him. However, the camaraderie was a poor substitute for the faithfulness she craved from those who cared for her. After the divorce, her mother emotionally abandoned her. She left Shirley in the care of various relatives off and on throughout her elementary school years. The aunts, uncles, grandfather, and even two step-fathers begrudgingly cared for her out of duty making her long for what she never knew – to have a relationship based on faithfulness.

As a child she grew up too quick looking for faithfulness by marrying at the age of 15 to escape a home where she was not wanted. Marriage confirmed what she already learned earlier in life that those who care for you are incapable of being faithful. Her

[1] A radical committal foundational pattern "refers to the early development of a leader in the foundational development phase who comes from a non-Christian background in which the leader is more or less processed into whatever values the environment supports (usually those of the secular society of the macro-context) and who makes a radical adult decision for Christ which involves a significant paradigm shift in terms of values and life-goals." When Shirley committed her life to the Lord, she did so as an adult coming from a non-Christian background. For more information see Dr. Clinton's **Leadership Emergence Theory**, chapter 11, page 344 in particular for the quote.

husband's lack of care and concern for her during her two pregnancies enraged her doctor who encouraged her to consider divorcing her husband. She followed through on that encouragement and filed for divorced shortly after the birth of her second son. Three years later in 1957, she married a second time.

During a difficult and dangerous fourth pregnancy in 1965, Shirley's doctor encouraged her to abort her child in order to save her life. Under that cloud of uncertainty and despair she was invited to attend a bridge game as a substitute for a lady member who could not attend. She remembers that game as though it was yesterday. She started sharing her troubles with Joan Lowery[2], a regular member of the bridge club.

"Don't let them take your baby. Jesus can help you have this baby and give you strength so that you can have and keep this baby," Joan said confidently. The fact that Joan kept reassuring Shirley that Jesus could help her, created the desire on Shirley's part to believe her. She found it intriguing that Joan talked about Jesus as though he lived next door to her.

When she went to see the doctor a few days later, she said, "Doctor Cherry, I'm going to have the baby."

Surprised he responded, "Well, I hope you know what you're doing."

Shirley remembers thinking, "Well, I don't but Joan does, and so I am going to step out on what she believes." She did. A couple of months later Charlie was born.

Before Charlie was born, Joan invited Shirley to attend church with her. Joan took Shirley to her Presbyterian Church. Unimpressed, Shirley told Joan that her Catholic Church was much better because they memorized their prayers instead of reading them like the pastor did at the Presbyterian Church.

Unperturbed Joan told Shirley on the way home, "There is a place that is just what you are looking for."

"How could she know what I am looking for when I don't even know what I am looking for," Shirley silently thought. That comment incubated in Shirley's mind for eight months before she called Joan one Sunday evening at 5 p.m. and said,

"Joan, do you remember what you said to me in the fall?"

"Yes, I do! Can you be ready in one hour? I'll pick up and take you to this small church," Joan responded.

There were about fifteen people attending the service that night. Even though Joan did not attend the church, she knew the pastor. The pastor was Irish and in his thick Irish brogue asked Joan if she would sing a song for everyone. She sang, "It's Real," a song about the doubts one has before accepting Jesus.

Infuriated by the words in the song Shirley thought, "She brought me here to humiliate me. If I ever get out of here I will never come back."

---

[2] Joan was a divine contact. According to Dr. Clinton a divine contact is "a mentor whom God brings in contact with a person at a crucial moment in his/her development in order to empower along the lines of one of the following empowerments: 1. to affirm either the person or some idea as legitimate and meeting with God's approval, 2. to encourage leadership potential, 3. to give guidance for some crucial decision, 4. to give perspective that will clarify some situation, 5. to link the person with some resource such as a person, finances, or information, 6. to link the person with some opportunity – for ministry, or for training, for personal development. In this case, Joan functioned to empower Shirley by giving guidance for the crucial decision she had to make in regards to aborting her baby. She also gave perspective on the situation and eight months later linked Shirley with a church service in which she accepted Christ.

After Joan finished singing and started down the stairs, the pastor said, "Can you sing us another song."

She walked back over to the pianist and asked if she could play "His Eye is on the Sparrow." As Joan sang the following words God's Spirit began to minister deep within Shirley's heart touching the longings of her heart.

Why should I feel discouraged, why should the shadows come,
Why should my heart be lonely, and long for heaven and home,
When Jesus is my portion? My constant friend is He:
His eye is on the sparrow, and I know He watches me;
His eye is on the sparrow, and I know He watches me.

Refrain

I sing because I'm happy,
I sing because I'm free,
For His eye is on the sparrow,
And I know He watches me.

Verse 2

"Let not your heart be troubled," His tender word I hear,
And resting on His goodness, I lose my doubts and fears;
Though by the path He leadeth, but one step I may see;
His eye is on the sparrow, and I know He watches me;
His eye is on the sparrow, and I know He watches me.

Verse 3

Whenever I am tempted, whenever clouds arise,
When songs give place to sighing, when hope within me dies,
I draw the closer to Him, from care He sets me free;
His eye is on the sparrow, and I know He watches me;
His eye is on the sparrow, and I know He watches me.[3]

During that song Shirley surrendered her entire life to Jesus – not just part of it. She said,

> I didn't come bits and pieces – I gave my total being to this man who had been faithful. No one in my whole life had ever been faithful. But here was a man that I could trust. When Joan sang, "His eye is on the sparrow and I know he watches me," I wept.[4]

---

[3] The song was originally written in 1905 by songwriters, lyricist Civilla D. Martin and composer Charles H. Gabriel.

[4] This quote is taken from a personal interview with Shirley Raper on June 2006. In fact, all of the personal quotes used in this Focused Life Biography by Shirley and other people are taken from personal interviews conducted in June, 2006, and in February, 2008. Other quotes are taken from written and email correspondence between those two dates. This is the first biography written on Shirley Raper's life which means all of the data at this time is raw.

That night while sitting on the pew Shirley thought, "I'm going to find out what he wants and I am going to do it."

Opening Illustration II:

Canaan in the Desert
Divine Contact and Contemporary Mentor
Age = 44

Shirley struggled for eleven years after accepting Christ going from one crisis to another. She read every self-help book she could find always looking for the answer to the new crisis she experienced. She would read the book, apply the principles to her life and still failed miserably. Because she gave herself wholeheartedly to the Lord at the time of her salvation, she would not give up this Christian life that seemed to fail her. During her early years as a Christian, the churches she attended taught that one could live life without sin by abiding according to a long list of do's and don'ts. It was this teaching that drove her to buy every new book that came out seeking to find the magic formula to give her success in her daily walk.

In 1976, on a bleak rainy September day Shirley lay down on her kitchen floor praying and sobbing, "God, this is it. The church, I'm sick of it and I've got no where to go and I don't know why I'm there and it's a horrible place."[5] Shirley was weary and worn out from trying to live up to everyone's expectations. Afterwards, she got up and drove to Charlottesville, ten miles away to the small Christian bookstore.

There were no other customers in the store when Shirley entered. The owner of the store was an Episcopalian priest. Because he was a priest she felt that he could give her some guidance. She told him how disgusted she was with the church and how she felt like quitting the church, but not God. After listening to her, he walked out from behind the counter and went and got Mother Basilea's book on **Repentance: The Joy Filled Life** and handed it to her.

"I think she has what you are looking for," he said.

That night Shirley devoured that book. She returned to the book store the next day and bought every book this woman wrote. There was something that distinguished these books written by this little German Lutheran woman from all of the other Christian self-help books written at that time Shirley had read.

In Germany, Mother Basilea formed an order called Canaan of the Desert. She formed a branch located in Arizona. After reading Mother Basilea's books, Shirley contacted her sisterhood and asked if she could visit them. They responded explaining that would not be possible at that time, but that they would put her on a waiting list. In the mean time, the sisters told Shirley about a retreat one of the sisters was leading in Saluda, North Carolina at an Episcopalian retreat center. This was the only retreat the sisters ever held on the East Coast. Shirley registered and attended. Sister Lucia (who later became Shirley's life-long mentor) came and taught on the love of Christ.

After attending the fall retreat a guest spot opened and they invited her to visit them in Arizona for one month. The sisters were warm and kind to Shirley. Their

---

[5] This quote was taken from a personal interview with Shirley Raper.

beautiful and melodious voices filled the convent. Shirley found them delightful. She shared how she felt like a "charging bull when she spoke in their presence." That perception caused her to constantly run back to her room at every chance to pray "Oh, please Jesus, make my voice like theirs." After praying she would go back and continue on with the job that they gave her to do. The sisters finally said to Shirley,

> And do you know, dear sister that the sound of your voice is the sound of your heart." Shocked, Shirley ran back to her room, and said, "Lord, erase my prayers. Change my heart." She had been praying for the "wrong end of the stick." She was praying for her voice to change when all the time it was her heart that needed changing.[6]

Commenting on her time at the convent in May 1977, Shirley later said, "That really was the beginning of everything that would shape my life. Up until then, my life was in crisis and fragmented." She was not able to join the order because of travel requirements. All sisters had to travel to Germany once a year to attend a national conference. Shirley could not do that with her family. However, she became a "Friend of Canaan of the Desert" and adopted their values and habits.

The Time-Line

There is a time-line at the end of this focused life biography (Appendix A) which breaks down Shirley's life into five main periods lasting 21years, 20 years, 9 years, 17 years, and the last PHASE which began in the year 2002 is at this time of writing still in progress. Mother Shirley is in her mid-seventies and still going strong. She continues to lead the religious order she established[7], she paints and teaches icon classes, plans and leads an annual spiritual retreat in the fall, leads the house church which meets in her home, leads and teaches a Monday night bible study for the young people who begged her to teach it, plus extends hospitality to the endless stream of visitors into her home. In the fall of 2008, the Syrian Orthodox Church will ordain Shirley into the priesthood. She is attending school now in the form of two week clusters of training by the Orthodox priests within this Syrian branch. I believe that Mother Shirley may be moving into a season of afterglow if her religious order continues to grow and expand.

The time-line is a generic or generalized time-line[8] due to the fact that Mother Shirley functioned as a type A and/or type B[9] lay leader for most of her life. It should be

---

[6] The quote is taken from an interview with Shirley in June, 2006.

[7] In the 1990's Mother Shirley established a religious order with her bible study group. For detailed information concerning her order see PHASE IV, subphase B.

[8] Dr. Clinton identified four types of time-lines. The generalized time-line is for lay leaders. The ministry time-line is for full time ministry leaders. For more information on time-lines see Dr. Clinton's LET (Leadership Emergence Theory) Manual. (1989:312) Shirley's ministry role was lay or part-time professionally for short periods of time. She spent her entire life after she became a Christian ministering to others but usually in a non-official capacity. For example, when she went to the Knoxville Women's Prison, she went not as a part of a church or with a nationally recognized Prison ministry, but on her own as a Cloistered Heart Sister. Her fall retreats are hosted by her often at a great personal cost even though she charges the going rate for retreats.

[9] Clinton identifies five types of leaders. Each type is defined by the level of influence capacity. The type A is defined by internal local influence and is considered to be a lay non-full time leader. Type B leader's influence is expanded to include external influence locally. The leader is still lay non-full time. Type C has local, district, and regional sphere of influence. This leader works full time. A type D leader's influence is at the regional or national level. The level E leader exerts influence at the national and international level. Throughout Shirley's life she

noted that even though she functions in the A and B category she does have the limited influence of a type D leader as she is considered to be the spiritual mother of some high ranking military officers stationed in the United States.

Mother Shirley entered ministry late in life as she accepted Christ as an adult. She did not grow up in a Christian home. Despite that fact, she did experience early destiny preparation through her childhood experiences which God later used to shape and forge her into the leader she was to become. Her major roles were two-fold: 1) as a mother-mentor to the young and the lowly all the way up to Generals in the military and 2) as a teacher in whatever role she found herself ranging from domestic to biblical to artistic venues. Her sense of humor, straight talk, and incredible love endeared her to those the church rejected. The characteristics that endeared her to those marginalized by the church were the same ones that frustrated those in the church leadership positions concerned with tradition and status quo.

Highly Condensed Biographical Narrative

The following running capsule is structured around five major time increments of Raper's life indicating the gradual development of her ministry through struggles, historical mentors, disappointments, and people.

BIOGRAPHICAL PHASE I: EMOTIONAL ORPHAN

(1933-1958) Age = Birth – 25

A. Longing to Belong

(1933-1948) Age = Birth – 15

Shirley Ann Linker was born on April 3, 1933 to Worth Hampton Linker and Roebiner Evens. She was an only child of her father and mother's marriage. Her father owned a truck stop/nightclub bar. Shirley grew up in a spiritual vacuum. Her parents were not affiliated with any denomination. Even though her mother did not practice Christian spirituality, she delved into dark spirituality by engaging in palm reading for the hired hands who worked the farm. This practice was not limited to her mother. During WWII her aunts used the Ojai Board to discern the fighting locations of her uncles. Shirley remembers participating with her aunts as they used the Ojai Board.

Shirley's parents divorced in 1940 when she was seven years old. After her parents divorced, her father entered the war as a Navy Sea Bee serving in the South Pacific. In addition to the emotional abandonment due to the divorce, she experienced actual physical separation due to the war through her father's enlistment. Adding to that, her mother abandoned Shirley by leaving her with relatives who did not want to care for her. The year her parents divorced, her mother suffered a mental breakdown at the age of 27. As a result, she was sent to live with relatives being shuffled from one relative's home to another.

---

traditional sense, she exerts influence at the national level through her mentoring relationships. For a more in-depth explanation refer to **The Mentor Handbook,** page "1-25."

For awhile she lived with her mother's parents. Shirley's grandfather hated her mother and took his anger out on Shirley. She remembers her grandmother as kind but strict. Her grandparents lived on an eleven hundred acre farm. No other children lived nearby. She lived with an alcoholic grandfather who did not like her which intensified the feelings of separation she experienced from her mother. As a child Shirley experienced great loneliness.

Shirley remembers attending school during World War II. In the fourth grade, every morning before class began all of the students sang patriotic songs. When Shirley's class-mates stated singing the music the words to the songs released an emotional torrent of tears rendering Shirley inconsolable. As a result, the teacher insisted that Shirley stand outside in the hallway while her class-mates sang because her wailing disrupted the class. During the war, she cut out articles detailing the battles by the Associated Press and compiled them into a scrapbook. At the time she did not understand that this emotional reaction to the military songs was a destiny preparation incident.[10] This was the beginning of her call by God to minister to those in the military.

When Shirley lived with her mother a neighbor provided much needed spiritual nurturing. Mr. Tyndall who lived two doors down had a daughter Shirley's age. Shirley went to the Southern Baptist Church with him and his daughter. Mr. Tyndall was the only father figure in Shirley's life at this time. She felt loved by him. Years later when she accepted the Lord, she immediately thought of Pop Tyndall and asked God to pull back the curtain in heaven so that he could see that she "made it." She always felt that he must have prayed for her.

At night Shirley propped her pillow up against the window so she could gaze at the stars. Despite the fact that her family did not attend church, and her mother and aunts engaged in occult practices, as a child Shirley often prayed to God. She would say, "God, are you up there? Would you do this or that for me?" And she discovered that God answered many of her prayers. This practice of praying and seeing numerous answers to prayer was an early indication of a future call to intercession.[11]

Shirley's mother modeled generosity and concern for the poor. On Saturdays, her mother would cook steaks for the Saturday night meal. Her mother always bought enough steaks for a poor family that lived several doors down from them. After her mother cooked the steaks she gave them to Shirley to take to the family. Shirley learned to cook like her mother. Her mother was also an expert seamstress. Often she would sew clothes for the poor people that she knew.

Years later at her mother's funeral, Shirley was shocked to discover the depth of her mother's generosity. As the people filed by her mother's casket each person shared how her mother met some urgent financial or material need. One person told Shirley that one Christmas her mother gave them money so that they could buy presents for their children. Another person recounted how her mother paid her daughter's dentist bill when

---

[10] This was a destiny preparation process item. Clinton defines a destiny preparation process item as "a grouping of process items concerning significant acts, people, providential circumstance, or timing, which hint at some future of special significance to a life and, when studied in retrospect, add firmness to a growing awareness of sense of destiny in a leader's life." (Clinton 1989:103) Part of Shirley's destiny included praying for the military, especially very high ranking military officers. This was the first in a series of incidences in her life hinting at her future role of intercessor for the military.

[11] This early shaping incident of Shirley praying and seeing results to her prayers is a destiny preparation process item. She prayed these prayers before knowing God as her personal Savior. This was the first hint that Shirley's life purpose was to intercede for strategic individuals in the military.

she did not have any money. Another family shared how one year her mother bought their children clothes for school. The list of generosity grew as each person filed by the casket recounting another act of kindness.

Her mother remarried two times. She had a son with her second husband. Her two step-fathers did not care for Shirley. Her home life was not pleasant. Her father remarried once. He had four sons with his second wife. The step-mother did not like Shirley and did not want Shirley to spend time with her father. As a result she had no place to call home. When she was a teenager she tried to escape her mother's home by spending time at her aunt's house in the summer. Her aunt introduced her to Bill Raper that summer, which some years later would become her second husband.

B. Rejected by Man

(1948-1954) Age = 15 – 21

When she was fifteen years old, she married Oren Verbal, an airline pilot. He was seven years older than her. Her whole motive for marrying Oren was to escape her mother's home. She longed to belong somewhere. Oren was not a good husband. Shirley had difficult deliveries for her two children with Oren. The first delivery was three days long. Oren did not come to the hospital to visit her for either delivery. Enraged, her doctor encouraged her to divorce her husband, not just because he did not come to the hospital for the birth of their children, but to protect her mental health. She took her doctor's advice and divorced Oren in 1954.

C. Accepted by Man

(1954-1958) Age = 21 – 25

Shirley was 21 years old when she divorced. She had a toddler and a baby. She re-met Bill Raper whom she met earlier as a teenager visiting her aunt one summer on the farm before her first marriage. Three years later she married Bill in 1957. Shirley said that he had integrity. Bill did not come from a Christian home either, even though he was a baptist.

She suffered a nervous breakdown when she was 25 years old. She remembers that she grew tired of "time" – time to get up, time to cook, time to go here or there. After the birth of Charlie, she was tired all the time. It was then that the doctor diagnosed her with no "tired mechanism." She would keep going and not realize that her body needed rest. To compensate, her doctor recommended that she either focus her attention in the home or at work, but not both. In reflection, she said that she would work at a job for two years and then quit because of exhaustion. Her love for people coupled with this missing "tired mechanism" resulted in many friendships wherever she worked.

Ministry Insights[12] from PHASE I

a. God Consciousness

At times God's leadership preparation begins long before the future leader is aware of his existence. Shirley's family of origin exhibited an unredeemed consciousness of the supernatural. They were aware of the supernatural realm and sought it outside of God's permitted parameters through the Oji Board and palm reading. While this awareness did not lead Shirley's family to the Lord, it indicated a generational heritage of supernatural sensitivity. Shirley spent time praying to God before she was a Christian. She received many answers to her prayers. One of her favorite memories is when she prayed for a bicycle during WWII. Bicycles were rare due to the war effort. She received the bicycle and knew that it was a direct answer to her prayer.

God began the long process of revealing himself to Shirley through answering her child prayers. It is interesting to note that the way in which Shirley sought God as a child (through prayer) revealed the future calling of God on her life.

b. Generational Strengths

Many of the strengths that comprise Shirley's ministry effective methodologies[13] are generational. Shirley had a call of leadership on her life whereas her mother and grandmother did not. The foundational natural talents under girding her future ministry remained consistent throughout her life. As Shirley's life is examined through the years, one can observe the generational trait of generosity, the natural talent of cooking and organizational skills woven throughout her various ministry endeavors,from restaurant evangelism to prison ministry to name a few. One of Shirley's guiding ministry values centers on the belief that leaders must practice generosity.

Strategic Development from PHASE I

The longings that developed the values leading to her eventual destiny, and the skills learned which later became effective methodologies were forged during this time in her life. Despite the fact that Shirley did not grow up in a Christian home, she had an acute awareness of God. Her parents divorced at an early age. She was shuffled from relative to relative during her mother's long absences. For all practical purposes she was an emotional orphan with no place to call home.

---

[12] A ministry insight is a discovery one makes after discovering personal giftedness or acquired skills while doing ministry in which the person identifies a method that enables effective ministry. Sometimes a ministry insight will result in a paradigm shift. For more information on a ministry insight refer to Clinton's **Strategic Concepts that Clarify a Focused Life,** p. 51.

[13] An effective methodology refers to "some ministry insight around which the leader can pass on to others the essentials of doing something or using something or being something, that is, a means of effectively delivering some important ministry of that leader which enhances life purpose or moves toward ultimate contribution". For more information on effective methodologies please refer to Clinton's **Strategic Concepts that Clarify a Focused** Life, p. 39. Shirley's effective methodologies center around the arts: her professional cooking skills, her ability to hear God in creative ways, dance, music, and painting among other non-artistic methodologies.

Leadership development did not begin during this PHASE of her life. However, strategic development did take place during this time period. The lack that she experienced from not having a mother to provide nurture and emotional support shaped her calling and destiny later in life. It also defined to whom she was called to minister to later in life – emotional orphans like her, the marginal and rejected ones by the church, both Christian and non-Christian and the military.

Some of her effective methodologies were also set in place during her childhood. Her mother and grandmother were excellent cooks. She excelled at that learned skill which she later used in hosting many spiritual retreats by preparing lavish banquets. Her mother was also facetious in teaching her how to set a proper table and having proper manners, which she later used in her celebration ministries.

BIOGRAPHICAL PHASE II: ADOPTED BY GOD

(1958 -1974) Age = 25 – 41

A. Accepted by God

(1958 – 1966) Age = 25 – 33

Shirley and her new husband both grew up in dysfunctional families. They made a commitment to each other that they would provide the family life for their children that they did not experience. She felt happy in her new marriage.

In 1965, Shirley was pregnant with her fourth child, a son. She was not doing well physically. Her doctor recommended an abortion to protect her life. It was against this backdrop that she was invited to attend a bridge game as a substitute player. While there she met Joan Lowery who was a Christian. Joan encouraged Shirley to keep her baby telling her that Jesus could protect both her and the child. Encouraged by Joan's faith, Shirley decided to keep her baby.

While Shirley was still pregnant, Joan invited Shirley to attend church with her. Shirley accepted her invitation but was negatively impressed by her church. Undisturbed, Joan told Shirley that she knew of a church Shirley would like. Confused that someone could know what she needed when she herself did not know; she filed that comment away in the recesses of her mind. Eight months later, she called Joan and asked if Joan would be willing to take her to that church.

Joan took her to a small Presbyterian Church. It was during the singing of the song "His Eye is On the Sparrow" that Shirley made a radical committal[14] to the Lord. After her decision to accept Christ as savior, she embarked on an aggressive study of scriptures.[15] She met with the Presbyterian pastor on a regular basis to ask him questions

---

[14] Refer to page 1, footnote 1 for a detailed explanation of a radical committal.

[15] Dr. Clinton identified six common characteristics of leaders who finish well. They are, 1. "They maintain a **personal vibrant relationship with God** right up to the end, and 2. They maintain a **learning posture** and can learn from various kinds of sources – life especially, and 3. They evidence **Christ likeness in character** as evidenced by the fruit of the Spirit in their lives, and 4. Truth is lived out in their lives so that **convictions** and promises of God are **seen to be real**, and 5. They leave behind one or more **ultimate contributions** (saint, stylistic practitioners, mentors, public rhetoricians, pioneers, crusaders, artists, founder, stabilizers, researchers, writers, promoters). For more information on Ultimate Contributions read Clinton's book **Strategic Concepts that Clarify a Focused Life**. 6. They walk with a growing awareness of a **sense of destiny** and see some or all of it fulfilled. For more information on the six characteristics see Dr. Clinton's book, **Focused Lives: Inspirational Life Changing Lessons from Eighth Effective Christian Leaders Who Finished Well**, p. 505. The intense study of the scriptures by Shirley shows how she

that resulted from her biblical studies. This pastor honored Shirley by answering her questions and not treating any questions as insignificant. He also honored her by asking if she would teach the elders in his church.[16] He recognized her teaching gifts. However, his decision reflected either an ignorance or non-application of the verse that states that new believers are not to be put in a place of leadership too soon. Shirley felt uncomfortable with this invitation and turned him down. What his invitation reflects is his recognition of her spiritual gifts and budding authority in teaching God's word.

Soon after Shirley and her husband Bill accepted the Lord, they were invited to attend the Keswick Conferences. They attended this particular conference every summer for ten years. The Keswick Conferences shaped Shirley spiritually giving her a solid foundation in the word. This conference introduced her to the Christian classics such as works by Watchmen Nee, Oswald Chambers, and Andrew Murray among others. She also had the opportunity to learn first hand from great Christian leaders and teachers in the United States during the 1970's, such as Richard Dehann, Paul Van Gorder, Theodore Epp, Vance Havner, and Robert McQuilkin.

B. Formed by God

(1966-1971) Age = 33 – 38

A few months after Shirley accepted the Lord she experienced her first demonic attack. The attack manifested physically through her gasping for breath. The first time she experienced this Bill, her husband took her to the hospital. She was unconscious for two days. The doctors ran every conceivable test to determine the cause of the attacks. All tests produced negative results. The attack always manifested in her body through the inability to breathe accompanied by shaking and jerking. During the first year of her salvation, Shirley spent approximately two nights in the hospital every week as a result of these attacks. She fell into a rhythm of thinking, "The doctor told me, 'there is nothing wrong with me, there is no reason why I can't breathe, so Lord, help me get my mind off of it."

One morning, after a particularly difficult night of not being able to sleep due to constant attack, Tiny, Shirley's laundry man, came to the door about 10 a.m. to deliver the dry cleaning. He handed her a little book. The little book had the word "Demons" written on it. Tiny was always giving Shirley tracks. She put the dry cleaning away and threw the track on the night stand before crawling back into bed hoping to fall asleep. That night as soon as the sun went down, the demons resumed their harassment. She thought she had to get her mind off of this because the doctor said there is nothing wrong. She reached over and grabbed the little book. Shirley decided to read it as her distraction. After reading it she thought, "Gosh, I wonder if this is what is wrong with me." She got down on her knees and said,

---

practiced the second common characteristic of leaders who finish well by maintaining a learning posture. This is a common trait through her life as she is always learning and applying what she learns practically to her life. She is currently studying to be ordained as a Syrian Orthodox priest in the fall of 2008.

[16] This was a ministry affirmation process item. Clinton defines a ministry process item as a special kind of destiny experience in which God gives approval to a leader in terms of some ministry assignment in particular or some ministry experience in general which results in a renewed sense of purpose for the leader." (Clinton 1989:267) In Shirley's case, this was a destiny experience hinting at the future role she would have in teaching/mentoring recognized leaders of the male gender. She did not recognize this invitation by the pastor as a destiny experience or as a ministry affirmation.

> Lord, if I've got this, if there are demons still around I want you to deliver me in your name like you delivered them in the olden times, in the name of Jesus, and if I don't have demons, then teach me to live with what I do have.

That was the beginning of the end of the demonic attacks. Shirley realized that this was not just an emotional problem. She shared what she read with her pastors, Brad and Joan. The frequency of the attacks decreased as they started to pray for Shirley. After six long years, relief finally came and the attacks ceased. This was a spiritual warfare process item.[17] Through this extended incident Shirley learned how to walk in spiritual authority.[18] At this time there was no cognition on her part that God was teaching her how to walk in spiritual authority. That cognition came later through dynamic reflection.[19]

God provided grace to Shirley throughout this six year struggle with the demons through a divine contact that became her historical mentor. She discovered the autobiography of Madame Guyon, a noble French woman.[20] Madame Guyon's life exerted a profound influence upon the shaping of Shirley's values and principles that defined her eventual leadership. She was drawn to the values and principles upon which Madame Guyon lived her Christian life.[21] The affinity between the two was so great that Shirley spent years praying that God would transform her life to mirror that of Madame Guyon. God answered that prayer. Madame Guyon was a woman leader during the 1600's when women were not permitted to be leaders. God's call on her life was counter-cultural and caused her a great deal of suffering as she obeyed God. It was no accident that Shirley was drawn to this historic woman leader. God had a similar call upon Shirley's life calling her into leadership in a Christian culture that for the most part did not permit or recognize women in positions of authority over men.

From all appearances God was training her in gender specific specialties. In 1968, Shirley started working as a teaching chef for the magazine, Southern Living. This was an early ministry assignment[22] in the marketplace which equipped her with needed

---

[17] Usually a spiritual warfare process item occurs during the growth phase of the leader, as was the case with Shirley. It took her six years to overcome these demonic attacks. As she grew in her understanding of God's word and in spiritual maturity the attacks gradually ceased. These experiences increased her spiritual authority dramatically. For more information on this particular process item refer to Clinton's **Leadership Emergence Manual**, p. 238.

[18] Spiritual authority refers "to a source of credibility from God that permits leaders to influence followers…Spiritual authority is not a goal but a byproduct." (Clinton 1988:255; 155) Spiritual authority is earned by obeying Christ and submitting to him and to those placed over us. Shirley never sought spiritual authority. It came as she sought the Lord.

[19] Dynamic reflection is "a two-fold thinking process which teaches how to correlate input ideas relevantly to experience and formation on the one hand, and on the other, the thinking processes which draw out from ministry experience, ideas that affect input and become new, more relevant input for the learner." For more information refer to Clinton's **Mentor Handbook**, p. 1-16. Dynamic reflection happened when Shirley received the booklet on demons and how to deal with them. She took that input and made it part of her value system. Spiritual authority resulted through the reflective process of applying God's word to her personal situation of demonic attacks.

[20] Madame Guyon became a historical mentor for Shirley. Clinton defines a historical mentor "as a person now dead whose life and ministry at least in part, is written in a biographical or autobiographical form, and is used as an example to indirectly impart skills, lessons of like and ministry, and values which empower another person." For more information on historical mentors refer to Clinton's book, **Mentoring Handbook**, p. 10-5. Shirley read all of the books that Madame Guyon wrote. In the fullest sense of the definition, Madame Guyon was Shirley's historical mentor.

[21] Reading Madame Guyon's autobiography was a literary process item for Shirley. According to Clinton it is the means God uses to "teach leaders lessons for their own lives through the writing of others." (Clinton 1989:184) Shirley was so taken by Madame Guyon's love for God that she prayed for years asking God to make her life mirror Madame Guyon's life.

[22] An early ministry assignment is more permanent than a ministry task (a one time ministry assignment) yet has the same basic pattern of entry, ministry, closure, and transition out of the ministry situation and through which God gives

skills for later ministry when she started her celebration processionals and as a point of contact with restaurant owners. This ministry assignment built upon her earlier training from her mother and grandmother in the art of cooking. Dr. Clinton calls that process "base plus advance."[23]

In the late 1960's during the Vietnam War, the small group in which Shirley belonged to ordered POW/MIA bracelets. Everyone took a bracelet with the commitment to pray for the missing military personnel listed on the bracelet. Shirley received the name of a Navy pilot shot down in 1969, over North Vietnam. God used the POW bracelet in bringing to pass Shirley's destiny to pray for the military. This was a destiny process item in which the bracelet would play a significant role later on. That process item is included in the Critical Incidents Chart.

It is easy to recognize the "no tired mechanism" at work in her life through her many jobs. In 1971, Shirley started working at the University of North Carolina. It was during this time that a move of God broke out upon the student population. She knew quite a few of the students and often had spiritual conversations with them. Some of the students began praying and asked God to give Shirley the spiritual gift of tongues. They did not tell her of their prayers. God answered and through an encounter with the Lord, she received the spiritual gift of tongues.

The first part of her leadership foundational training was complete. She was now positioned to enter the second phase of her leadership development. Now that God had formed her into his image, she was soon to discover that man would reject what God treasured.

C. Rejected by Man

(1971-1974) Age = 38 – 41

One summer while attending the Keswick Conference a man walked across the room to where Shirley was sitting. It was Robert McMillen. He knelt down beside her and proceeded to give her the following word, "You will be a Mother in Israel of hundreds and yea thousands." This word disturbed Shirley as she was thinking in the natural and did not want anymore children. Her friend, Jackie sitting next to her laughed. This word proved to be directive giving greater clarification to her destiny as a mother to everyone needing a mother.

All mothers teach, whether it be explicit or implicit through modeling as her children watch her. This was true of Shirley also. Her reputation as a teacher grew. A local pastor of a church Shirley did not attend asked if she would fill in for him while he was sick with the flu. He told her that she could not preach because that was not allowed but that she could give her testimony to the congregation. His request was a ministry affirmation process item as he recognized her ability to teach with spiritual authority.

---

new insights to the leader so as to expand influence, capacity, and responsibility toward future leadership. This ministry task of being a teaching chef at Southern Cooking gave Shirley credibility and influence later in life with owners of different restaurants she frequented on a regular basis.

[23] This concept discovered by Dr. Clinton refers to the process where upon someone keeps developing upon the base unit, be it knowledge or of another commodity. In this incidence, the base refers to what Shirley learned as a child. The advance refers to building upon that initial knowledge from childhood when she started working at Southern Cooking as a teaching chef.

This affirmation was yet another destiny experience for her revealing a future calling upon her life as that of a pastor to both genders. Not all pastors were mature like this pastor who was not threatened by her spiritual authority.

Shirley and Bill attended the baptist church in town. She was a successful Sunday school teacher to the young married couples. The church embraced the traditional belief that women were not allowed to teach men, only women and children. However, this baptist church made an exception because they recognized her ability to teach with authority and observed the fact that when she taught more people attended the church. Her intent after she received the spiritual gift of tongues was not to discuss it with anyone at church out of respect of the church's doctrinal position of not speaking in tongues. However, people noticed a change in her and pressed her for what happened. Reluctantly she shared how she received the spiritual gift of tongues and the results of that gift upon her life. At first, the elders did not know what to do with her. She was a successful teacher who taught with authority and was very popular.

The elders dealt with the "problem" by removing her from the young married class which had grown from nothing to 30 people within a year. They assigned her to the high school class. Within a short time, the young married couples and people from other classes started attending the high school class. Frustrated the elders removed her from that class to the least desirable class – the ladies over fifty years of age. The elders did not expect people to leave the assigned classes in order to attend her class. Shirley was more popular than all of the male teachers in the church. Finally, the elders held a meeting and decided to kick Shirley out of the church. Her husband, Bill was an elder sitting in at the meeting. He told the elders that would not be necessary as he would take his family elsewhere. One young married man stood up to the elders by telling them that it was inconsistent for them to ignore the scriptures when it was to their benefit but then, to follow scriptures when they found it convenient.

God's call upon Shirley's life is gender specific; she is called to be a mother to the motherless. Her role as a leader and influencer was not gender biased. God called her to the role of leader to both men and women. It is true that the word she received about being a mother in Israel was gender specific, but the role of leader and the sphere of influence it would one day include, was not gender specific. Shirley felt that the gender excuse used by many male leaders was not the real reason for her rejection. She felt that it was a cover-up reason for other dynamics at work. The elders and pastor at the baptist church allowed her to teach even though she was a woman who also had the spiritual gift of tongues. It was when it became clear that she was more popular than the male teachers through a church-wide vote that it became imperative for her to leave. The elders used the gender and cessationist[24] reasons for her expulsion.

This was the first incident Shirley experienced in which she felt the rejection of man upon the call of God on her life. Not only did she suffer rejection by those who were of the non-charismatic persuasion, but within a few years, she would suffer greater rejection by those of the charismatic community. It was through negative shaping incidences like this that God answered her prayer allowing her life to mirror the attitudes and values that Madame Guyon embraced and taught. Madame Guyon accepted all events as from the hand of God. Shirley was learning how to do the same.

---

[24] Cessationism refers to the belief that certain spiritual gifts ceased to operate after the death of the original twelve disciples of Jesus died.

Ministry Insights from PHASE II:

a. The Study and Application of God's Word Brings Life

After Mother Shirley accepted the Lord she had a deep hunger to know everything that this man taught. She bought a bible and began a life-long pursuit of studying scriptures in order to live out the principles in her life. In addition to personal study she also pursued other training throughout her life. At the age of 75 she is studying for the Priesthood within the Syrian Orthodox Church. One cannot lead apart from knowing God's word.

b. Celebrate!

In 1969 while Shirley watched a football game with her four children she experienced a revelation from God about the importance of celebrating the majesty and splendor of the Lord. The half-time show was spectacular. She observed how people took the time and energy to produce a program in which the arts were used to express pageantry for a national pastime. Immediately she was able to translate what she saw into the sacred by grieving over the fact that the church does not celebrate the splendor of God with the same enthusiasm as was expressed during the football game.

Responding to this void within the church, Shirley organized dance troupes, a tambourine team, and a sword team for men. The dance teams designed modest but ornate costumes for the different teams. These dance teams participated in processionals for well-known Christian organizations such a Gwen Shaw and the End Time Handmaidens, the Lydia group, and conferences and churches.

Over time this ministry insight about the importance of celebrating morphed into the annual spiritual retreats Shirley hosts each year with the sisters in her sisterhood. She views these times of celebration as covenant renewing times with the Lord for all of the participants. There is little teaching. The retreats centers on celebrating the presence of the Lord with majesty and splendor. The result is that much healing takes place without the formal inner healing techniques. Often the attendants are set free just by being in the presence of the Lord where his splendor and majesty is celebrated.

c. Historical Mentors

From early childhood Shirley loved to study. This trait was not nurtured by her mother; it welled up from deep within Shirley. From Clinton's extensive research he discovered that leaders who finish well have many mentors including historical mentors. During this PHASE Shirley discovered Madam Guyon. She read her biography and then the other works by her. Shirley was able to take the principles that guided Madame Guyon's life and apply it to her own. The reading of Madam Guyon's life was a Literary Processing Item.

Shirley resonated with the passion this woman had for God, the incredible desire she had to love all, and her voracious spiritual appetite. Her identification with this woman from the 1600's was so strong that Shirley embarked upon a prayer begging God to make her just like her historical mentor.[25] God did. It took her whole life, but God

---

[25] The fact that Shirley was attracted to Madam Guyon demonstrates the "Like attracts like" principle. Clinton writes that there is an intuitive attraction between aspiring leaders and mature leaders because of the "like attracts like" principle. Shirley's life will demonstrate the validity of that principle. (1989:360)

answered her prayer. Shirley's struggles paralleled much of the suffering by Madame Guyon. A great deal of Madame Guyon's suffering stemmed from the religious leaders of the day jealous of her gifts. They were incensed that she would do what was culturally unacceptable – speak and teach with spiritual authority exerting her influence internationally. This made her a type E leader.[26] One difference is that Shirley did not spend time in prison for her beliefs, but that is due to the country and the prevailing laws of the United States. God used Madame Guyon counter-culturally, just as he was beginning to do with Shirley in this second PHASE of her life. Shirley was no longer an emotional orphan. She was adopted by God and now she was free to enter into the next PHASE of her life in which she would be nurtured by God.

Ministerial and Spiritual Development from PHASE II

Shirley's vow to find out what Jesus wanted and then to do it, propelled her into an intensive course of study of His life for the rest of her life. This training was in line with her destiny even though she was not cognizant of that fact. Every leader needs to be trained. Shirley's training in PHASE II was primarily two-fold, spiritual (dealing with leadership character issues) and ministerial (dealing with leadership insights). As a leader soon to receive the call of spiritual mother and confirmations of pastoral leadership, she needed to grow in her understanding of God's word. Gaining mastery of God's word in turn gave her the necessary tools to deal with some spiritual and character issues in her life. Her studies and overcoming the demonic attacks increased her spiritual authority. As a pastor/teacher she needed spiritual authority to teach and preach God's word powerfully. Her doctor's diagnosis that her body lacked a "tired mechanism," facilitated the gaining of needed ministry skills. This set her in a rhythm of changing jobs often, always taking a rest-break between each job. This developed her passions as she worked in a wide variety of jobs in different fields. This exposure allowed her destiny to slowly unfold according to God's time-table.

[26] Dr. Clinton defines a type E leader as someone who is in full-time ministry exerting national and international influence. (Clinton 1989: 360)

BIOGRAPHICAL PHASE III: NURTURED BY GOD

(1974-1983)

A. Church without Walls

(1974-1977) Age = 41 – 44

Until now, Shirley viewed the church as the actual building. After she was kicked out of the baptist church she experienced a paradigm shift.[27] As a displaced Christian, she realized physical buildings do not constitute the "church." Believers comprised the church, not the buildings. This paradigm shift allowed her to view the church in a fluid context – the church had no walls!

The paradigm shift happened slowly as Shirley and her husband became more involved in home groups and less formally involved in the organized church. After she was kicked out by the baptist church she and her husband attended many different church denominations as they moved from state to state following Bill's work assignments. While they never stopped attending church, they became more involved in the home group movement. Shirley was the leader of the home groups that met in their home.

People were attracted to her because of her ability to teach with spiritual authority. Pastors of different denominations would call Shirley and ask her to fill in for them while they were away on vacation or when they were sick. Both men and women recognized her spiritual authority and granted her access to teaching venues, even those off limits to women at that time in Church history.

God prepared Shirley for the negative processing incident of being kicked out of the baptist church a few years prior while she attended the Keswick Conference. One of the speakers, Dr. Van Gorder brought his books on a subject he termed Charismatic Confusion. He planned to speak on that subject and sell his books on that same subject. The conference director, Robert McQuilkin told Van Gorder that the Keswick Conference was a "broad umbrella" and that nothing should be taught that would bring division there because it was an ecumenical gathering. Dr. Van Gorder was given the choice of selecting another topic to teach or not to teach at all.

Shirley studied his response to Robert McQuilkin's directive. He never argued to prove his point. He put his books away and selected another topic to teach. He never criticized or appeared to exhibit any negative attitudes toward that incident. He was respectful toward Robert McQuilkin and toward the ecumenical parameters guiding the Keswick Conference. Observing how Dr. Van Gorder graciously handled that incident taught Shirley how to respond to rejection by those in leadership.

The ecumenical tenor of the Keswick Conference influenced her church wanderings in the years to come. She never wandered from God, but she and her husband did wander from church denomination to church denomination as they moved

[27] The experience of being kicked out of the baptist church for speaking in tongues and being more popular than the male teachers produced a paradigm shift for Shirley. A shift happens after a series of incidents force the leader to adopt a new perspective replacing an old perspective. Before this negative processing item of being expelled from the Church, Shirley viewed the Church as being connected with the actual building. In order for her to move forward with her calling to the marginalized and rejected, she needed to embrace a contradictory paradigm of understanding the Church not in terms of the actual building, but in terms of the Body of Christ comprised of individual believers.

from one geographical location to another. She learned a valuable lesson from her historical mentor, Madame Guyon. Madame Guyon wrote that it was important to "glean wherever one goes.[28]" Shirley applied that value to all of her church wanderings even to the churches that kicked her out in the past and those churches who would kick her out in the future.

Shirley studied God's word not to gain knowledge but to actually apply it to her life. After she was kicked out of the baptist church, she grew weary and discouraged over the fact that she could not find a church where people actually applied God's word to their lives both when it was convenient and not convenient. Through this time of discouragement God led Shirley to the writings of a German Lutheran woman, Mother Basilea. Shirley read all of her works, discovered that she had a sisterhood living in Arizona, and within a short time was invited to live in community with the sisters for one month. This was her first exposure to a community living by faith. It was here that she was able to observe Christian values and principles lived out. God used this month of living in community as preparation for a few years later when God arranged for her to form her own community.

God nurtured Shirley primarily through non-church structures during this sub-phase of her life. She gained a foundational understanding of scripture by attending the Keswick Conference every summer. She was able to "build on the base plus advance principle"[29] on this knowledge by spending a month with the Lutheran sisters living in community in Arizona. By observing the Lutheran sisters, Shirley observed what Biblical principles and values looked like in action. This ability to glean wherever she went guarded her heart attitude from becoming bitter. The key was the ability to learn how to glean even when she was dishonored by man. It was foundational in discovering that the Church had no walls.

The Consequences of Sin

When Shirley first became a Christian in 1966 she thought that one of the first things God would ask her to give up was her smoking, because in her mind smoking was the worse thing she did. She was wrong. Upon reflection she said that there were so many other issues in her life more serious than smoking that God wanted to address first. Eight years after her salvation God was ready to deal with her habit of smoking. Through the years she tried unsuccessfully to give up smoking. Finally, she told God that she tried and that she knew He wanted her to quit, but it was not possible for her to quit.

Early one morning before her daughter Holly went to school, they read a verse from Psalms, "When I am afraid, I will trust in Him." (Psalm 56:3 KJV) Holly 13 years old owned a horse and decided that she wanted to ride her horse before she left for school. While riding, the horse stumbled throwing Holly to the ground and crushed her. She was rushed to the hospital critically injured. While Shirley sat in the hospital hallway this thought flashed through her mind, "You've told me that you can't quit smoking. Now I've touched something that you do love. Lay them (the cigarettes) down

---

[28] The quote is from Mother Shirley. The saying is distilled from Madame Guyon. Madame Guyon believed that one should always learn from every situation – good or bad.

[29] This principle refers to the process of continually developing upon what one already has. In this case, by spending time with the Lutheran sisters, Shirley added to the knowledge she had from her previous studies of God's word.

and I will raise her up." Stunned, Shirley was faced with the consequences of her own sin afflicting the life of someone close to her.

All night long, the pastor of the Foursquare Church, she and Bill attended paced back and forth in a hallway praying the same words over and over again, "Glory to God...Glory....Glory to God." The verse that Shirley and Holly read the morning before the accident came back to Shirley repeatedly comforting her. Reflecting back on this critical processing incident[30] Shirley said:

> She paid the price for me because I couldn't give them (cigarettes) up. I tried everything I could and finally I said to God, "I can't do this." I will always love her (Holly) because she paid such a price. You know the wonderful part; she does not remember the accident. She doesn't remember anything about it. For two weeks she could not speak. All she can remember is that verse of scripture we read the morning before the accident, "What time I am afraid I will trust in him." God was with us. Let me tell you something. You may say, "That was terrible." I don't believe that...Was it horrible? Yes! For her it was horrible, but he took the memory of it away. He raised her up and cured me (of smoking). There is nothing about it that is not good.[31]

Shirley never blamed God for Holly's accident. Her response to Holly's accident was influenced by the writings of Madame Guyon. Dr. Clinton teaches that leaders who finish well have many mentors. After Holly's accident, Shirley met a group of new mentors who modeled the unbiased and manifest love of Christ.

New Mentors: Mother Basilea and the Sisters of Canaan in the Desert

Leaders who finish well have many mentors. It was time for Shirley to find another mentor to deposit into her life like Madame Guyon did. In the fall of 1976, Shirley was ready to give up on the church but not God. God used her anguish to introduce her to the teachings of a German Lutheran woman, Mother Basilea. Her teachings resonated deep within Shirley's spirit at a time when she felt isolated and discouraged over the lack of genuine Christian charity and obedience within the church. She bought every book this woman wrote. Not only did she read her books, but she studied them and incorporated Mother Basilea's values into her own life making her a contemporary mentor.

The second critical incident recounts how Shirley discovered Mother Basilea and the Sisters of Canaan in Arizona. Years earlier Madame Guyon became her historical mentor. Now God was ready to give Shirley a contemporary mentor who would complement the teachings she gleaned from Madame Guyon, in addition to a spiritual mother through Sister Lucia. Sister Lucia remained Shirley's spiritual mother until she died in 2006.

In May 1977, Shirley had the privilege of living with the sisters who formed the Arizona chapter of Canaan in the Desert. The sisters lived life by faith. They never publicized their needs. Everyday they prayed and asked God to give them the food that

---

[30] Crisis processing incident: Clinton describes this incident as "a special intense situation of pressure in human situations which are used by God to test and teach dependence." (Clinton 1989:210) This crisis incidence happened in Shirley's general ministry phase on her time-line. Through this she learned the importance of depending upon God and never again to tell God that one cannot depend upon him.

[31] Shirley learned a difficult lesson through Holly's horse accident. She learned that if we do not deal with our sin issues they will cause harm to others. Her line of thinking is scriptural. Throughout scripture we read of the consequences that others suffered because of sin in another's life. Some examples are Lot and his two surviving daughters after Sodom was destroyed, King Saul, King David and many more.

they needed for that day. It never failed but that someone in the community would come by and give eggs, bread, or bags of groceries.

One day during Shirley's stay with the sisters they ran out of food. No one panicked. Instead all of the sisters gathered together in one room. To Shirley's amazement the gathering was not to pray and ask God to supply their need, it was to spend time repenting and confessing any grievances the sisters held against one another. One sister confessed that she was upset with another sister for something she did. Another sister confessed holding a grudge. After all the sisters repented and their relationships were restored, there was a knock on the door as someone from the community brought food to the convent. The individual from the community had no way of knowing that the sisters had just finished repenting to one another. He did not know that they had run out of food earlier that day and that the sisters already missed one or two meals.

This critical incident modeled the importance of repentance within the church community and the ramifications when grievances are held and not confessed. Shirley learned that this was standard operating procedure for the Sisters of Canaan in the Desert. Anytime their food donations or other donations ceased, the sisters gathered together to repent to one another of the grievances that they held against one another. It never failed that once their confession was complete, the donations resumed. This incident allowed Shirley to witness first hand how forgiveness is connected with the blessings of God and how unforgiveness blocks the blessings of God.

B Holy Mathematics

(1977-1983) Age = 43-50

Shirley taught a bible study once a week at the local mall. By now she earned a reputation of being a powerful bible teacher speaking with authority. A woman, Jackie started attending her bible study in 1977. Jackie worked at the mall. The bible study grew. After a short while some of the husbands told their wives to stop attending the bible study. They said that Shirley did not have a spiritual covering since she did not have the covering of any man. Without that spiritual covering her teaching could not be trusted they told their wives.

Heartbroken over the accusations of these men she told her husband, Bill. He told her that he would be her covering which according to what these men said would make her teaching legitimate. Not satisfied Shirley went to the Lord in prayer. The last thing she wanted was to teach without spiritual covering. Shirley was never defensive in her Christian journey.[32] When people accused her of being something her constant posture was, "I don't mind being one; I just don't want to remain one." She asked God why he would have her teach when she did not have a spiritual covering. She said that God impressed upon her that these men were not her spiritual covering but that God was her spiritual covering. That settled the matter for her.

After a year of attending the bible study at the mall, Jackie and her husband decided that they wanted to move closer to Shirley and Bill so that they could attend their home group. Jackie and Frank sold their home. They were unable to find anything to buy. When escrow closed they were forced out of their home with no place to go.

[32] As stated earlier, a leader who finishes well is one who is teachable, which is the second of the six characteristics.

to go. Shirley and Bill told them that they could move in with them for a few months until they were able to find a place to buy. Bill and Shirley fixed up the garage to make it livable for Frank and Jackie.

At the same time, another family Andy and Katcha Ring, Wycliffe missionaries to Ghana, moved into Shirley and Bill's one bathroom home with their three children. In addition, the Raper's also invited a young mother escaping an abusive husband with her three children, and a young man who tried to commit suicide. Within a couple of months nineteen people lived in their one bathroom house. Shirley never planned to go into community; however, it was God's design for her leadership development. During this year new paradigms were discovered, friendships forged, and healing resulted in the lives of those nineteen people.[33] Some of these people became life-long friends of Shirley.

About one year later, during a mid-week meeting at Lamb's Chapel, a visitor, Don Kaspersen prophesized by saying "There comes a time when a baby needs to be weaned." Don saw a picture in his mind of a baby nursing with hands pushing the baby away. From that visual impression, he sensed that it was time for the people to find their own way and move out of community. Within a month everyone moved out including Shirley and Bill. They sold the house and moved to Black Mountain, North Carolina.

One of Shirley's favorite sayings is "With every loss there is a gain." Over the course of two years beginning in 1982, Bill made some bad business decisions which eventually lost him and Shirley $256,000 and their home. Shirley said,

> We went from the country club section to a four room shack because he made some bad choices. It was a small price to pay for what we gained. *It was a small price to pay* (she repeated that phrase for emphasis). I've never missed one dime of it, not one dime because it brought him to his senses!

Shirley recounted how God orchestrated this loss to gain her husband's attention. Now that he had his attention, God was ready to enlarge Shirley's physical and spiritual family.

Ministry Insights from PHASE III:

a. Upward Mentors

According to Dr. Clinton, leaders who finish well have many upward mentors. An upward mentor is someone who is farther along in the process and mentors others. Shirley had three significant upward mentors over the course of her life. The first was her historical mentor, Madame Guyon. Second, Mother Basilea became her contemporary mentor and third, Sister Lucia became her spiritual mother. She met her in 1977, when she went and stayed with the Sisters in Canaan in the Desert for one month. Sister Lucia remained her spiritual mother until she died in 2006.

b. Ice Cream Parlor of 47 Flavors

Sister Lucia from Canaan of the Desert became a life long spiritual mother-mentor to Shirley. One day Shirley asked Sister Lucia how the sisters could work with

---

[33] This experience broadened and deepened her understanding of what comprised the Church. This group of nineteen people lived the Church in an everyday context which was different from viewing the Church as a place one goes to once or twice a week.

diverse, different, and sometimes difficult people. She responded, "Aye, dear Shirley, different flavors of ice cream in the parlor – it's just not our flavor. I don't have to worry that I don't like pistachio." The Sisters of Canaan of the Desert worked with many diverse people embracing many different doctrines whether they approved of their methods or not. They learned how to pray for and work with all without being critical or judgmental.

Shirley took this illustration and made it foundational in her life and to her teachings. She applied this teaching to her life by not criticizing other Christians who embraced teachings or forms of Christianity differently from what she embraced. It was this teaching that allowed her to reach out to those Christians marginalized and/or hurt by the organized Church. The ice cream illustration embraces a counter-cultural paradigm of not criticizing those who minister out of a different set of values or doctrines. This value enabled Mother Shirley to glean from every denomination with whom she associated regardless of how the people in a particular church treated her.

c. No Losses in God

Over the course of two years from 1982 until 1983, Bill made a bad financial decision which caused them to lose over $256,000. They lost this amount in two years, as well as their house. Yet, Mother Shirley did not view these as losses, since it was these disasters that caused her husband to get right with God. She said this was the "happiest day of my life" because of what was spiritually gained.

d. Accept Your Circumstances as from God

This is another teaching of Madame Guyon. Mother Shirley was able to embrace many crosses and as a result, she never stopped growing nor did she become bitter toward those who hurt her. She said, "When it (circumstances) comes in the form of a cross or pain embrace it." It is evident that this particular insight enabled her to view any loss not as a loss but as God's shaping for what was to come.

Strategic Development from PHASE III

God removed the glass ceilings that would have limited Shirley's leadership, sphere of influence, and spiritual authority through some extreme circumstances. Through Dr. Clinton's research he identified six barriers to finishing well.[34] In PHASE III, God addressed barrier one, the use and misuse of finances, barrier two, the abuse of power, and barrier five, family issues. God removed barrier one and five when Bill lost the $256,000. Shirley recognized God's hand in the endeavor and blessed the loss. The course correction in Bill's life as a result of losing the money meant that Shirley would be able to continue growing into her destiny. God continued to address the third barrier, abuse of power by allowing her to grow up under those who abused power so that she

[34] The six barriers to finishing well are as follows: 1. the use and abuse of finances, 2., the abuse of power, 3., pride, 4., illicit relationships (sex), 5., family issues, and 6., plateauing. For a more in-depth study refer to Clinton's book, **Focused Lives**, p. 499-500.

could learn how not to abuse. With these glass ceilings[35] removed, Shirley was free to move into the next PHASE of her calling, motherhood to all.

BIOGRAPHICAL PHASE IV: MOTHER TO ALL

1983-2002 Age 50 – 69

A. A Mother to the Abused

(1983-1987) Age = 50 – 54

After Bill's financial loss, he and Shirley moved into a small run-down four room house they owned. A year later, they sold that house and planned to move into a retirement home. The Raper's invited their two grandsons to stay with them while they moved. They drove over to pick up their grandsons. They were excited at the prospect of spending time with their grandsons for two weeks as that was the time-limit imposed by the retirement center for non-resident guests. When they arrived at their daughter Holly's home, they were appalled to see their oldest grandson, three years old badly beaten by his daddy during a fit of rage. Quick thinking Shirley told Holly that they would take the boys in. They invited Holly to move in with them if she wanted. There was one problem with their decision to take in their grandsons; the retirement's home strict policy on no children living there. That meant that now they had no place to live!

Shirley and Bill were faced with a dilemma. They had sold their house, their possessions were packed in a truck, but they could not allow their grandsons to continue to live with the father who almost killed one in a fit of rage. They drove to Sparta, Tennessee and spent the night in a motel. The next day they went to a real estate office and the agent happened to have a small house for sale. In the course of one day they went from retiring to becoming parents to the abused!

This sub-phase initiated transition on multiple levels. The circumstantial situation in which Shirley found herself mirrored God's call upon her life. She took in her grandsons rescuing them from an abusive setting. This action reflected this new phase of her life in which God transitioned Shirley to become a mother to the suffering and the rejected.

Late one night Shirley read Genesis 35:1-11.[36] The story about Jacob getting rid of the idols from his house and changing clothes impacted Shirley. She felt that God wanted her to get rid of her jewelry and fashionable clothes. She could not shake the revelation that God wanted her to wear a gray habit similar to what nuns wear. Clothes, jewelry, and make-up were important to her. Once she knew for certain in her mind that God wanted her to change her clothes for him, she did it quickly. In the course of one week, Shirley sold all of her designer and custom tailored clothes, her shoes, and her expensive jewelry. In all, she netted $4,000 from the sale. At first, her children, friends

[35] A glass ceiling is a phrase that refers to the limits placed on an individual preventing advancement or promotion due to one's gender, race, or religion. The word "glass" refers to the real, but invisible nature of the limit. It becomes visible only if the individual tries to advance beyond the invisible limitations.

[36] A word process item is when God uses a verse or several verses to bring about a change in direction or a course of action. (Clinton 1989a:182)

and strangers ridiculed her. However, Bill never made fun of her of nor did he ever feel ashamed of her decision to wear a gray habit. It was when she started wearing the gray habit people both young and old began calling Shirley, "Mother Shirley." The word spoken to her years before by Robert Mc Millen and Rick Joyner was coming to pass.

After living in Sparta for one year, she and Bill decided to move to Kentucky. Their daughter Holly stayed on in Sparta, but they took their two grandsons with them. Shirley's grandsons, Joseph and Elijah would continue to live with Shirley and Bill for five more years. While in Kentucky, Mother Shirley co-hosted a once a month radio program called On the Front Porch. It was in a dialogue format with the owner of a Christian radio station discussing current issues. One morning while Mother Shirley was speaking on the radio, a young army Lieutenant listened. So impressed by what he heard, he called the radio station and requested to meet the woman who spoke. This meeting was the beginning fulfillment of her call to pray for the military.

B. Mother Shirley of the Franciscan Order of the Cloistered Heart

(1987-1991) Age = 54 – 58

Shirley had a sense that God wanted her to return to the Catholic Church and apologize for her judgmental attitudes toward the Church of her heritage. She went to the Catholic Church in town and repented to the priest – not in a booth – but in his office as she shared her life journey with him. He blessed her and accepted her repentance. He welcomed her to attend the services as God directed her.

While living in Kentucky Shirley met with several other women on a regular basis to pray for their children. They so wanted to see their children accept the Christian values as their own. They felt that the best way to accomplish that goal would be to go into intentional community by forming a sisterhood. They formed the "Franciscan Order of the Cloistered Heart. In order to learn about the Franciscan way of life they asked a Franciscan priest to come and teach them as novitiates. Many of the sisters who joined Mother Shirley's order were Protestants and all were or had been married at one time in their lives.

Mother Shirley taught a bible study while living in Kentucky. In 1987, some of the Christian pastors from the area wanted to start a new ministry and invited Mother Shirley to participate in their endeavor. These Christians leaders were immature. They were passionate about this ministry endeavor. They were passionate about this ministry opportunity. They recognized the high level of spiritual authority Shirley had. Unfortunately, their immaturity did not prepare them for Mother Shirley's response. She prayed about the endeavor and felt that God did not want her to participate. Her refusal to participate angered these leaders of the surrounding churches. They viewed her refusal as divisive. They did not understand that her non-participation was not divisive nor a rejection of their ideas. The pastors from the Vineyard and other Charismatic churches agreed to jointly denounce Mother Shirley as a Jezebel on the same Sunday for her refusal to join them in their endeavor. They instructed their people not to have anything to do with her.

The church Shirley and Bill attended kicked her out. Prior to this decision, her husband Bill warned the pastor by telling him "to do what you have to do, but be careful." Six months later, Bill's job moved him again to another state. Within a few years all but one pastor came to a bitter end. The only pastor who did not come to a bitter end sought forgiveness from Mother Shirley for his role in the matter. Many of the offending pastors fell into adultery and left the ministry.

A short time later in 1989, Mother Shirley and Bill moved back to Black Mountain, North Carolina. They went into community and bought four adjoining farms. Sister Charlene lived on one of the farms, their son and daughter-in-love, Myrrh (Mother Shirley does not use the phrase in-law but in-love) moved onto another farm. It was during this time that they began to minister at the local military base.

A short time after this incident God blessed Mother Shirley by restoring to her one of her passions. Years prior Mother Shirley felt impressed by the Lord to surrender her artistic abilities to his direction. She is musically and artistically gifted. She loved to paint. She sensed the Lord would not let her paint because it would be a distraction from her pursuit of him at that time, she grieved but obeyed. Finally in 1991 she felt released by God to resume her painting by learning the art of icon painting[37]. This artistic endeavor became a spiritual discipline. She studied the lives of each saint she painted. She turned each icon painting into a time of prayer asking God to transform her into the likeness of the biblical or early Christian saint she painted.

C. Mother to All Denominations

(1991-1998) Age = 58 – 65

Wherever Shirley lives she teaches a bible study attracting men and women of different denominations. Her principle of "glean wherever you go" allowed her to attend many different denominations and despite how the denomination treated her, she would have something positive to say about each denomination. She once said,

> Glean everywhere you go. Everywhere you can – the beautiful things that are in your life! I glean from the Orthodox, their great love, I glean from the Charismatics and the Pentecostals the gifts of the Holy Spirit, and I glean from the Baptists, their great, great love of salvation, as they want to see everyone saved. I glean from the Methodists; their women are the greatest homemakers of the world, and the best cooks you've ever seen. I glean from the Catholics the fact that children are a blessed reward from the Lord, so if you're not stupid, you can glean from everyone, and you put that together to the glory of God.[38]

She accepts all people who hunger to know more of God regardless of their denomination affiliation. Her posture allows the acceptance of Sisters that are not Catholic.

Mother Shirley and Pops, as her husband Bill came to be known, retired to a farm near Mosheim, Tennessee. She called the farm The Shulamite's House taking the term

[37] Iconography is the art of painting icons. Christian icons date from the early church. An icon is a painted picture of saints from the Bible or early Christian saints. It is a precise art regulated by many rules.

[38] This quote was taken from a taped conversation with Shirley in June 2006.

from the Song of Solomon, her core book of the Bible.[39] While living near Mosheim she started a catering business named "Poverello's Joy" after St. Francis of Assisi. It means "poor little one." The name that she selected is a reflection of her call to the poor and marginalized. Mother Shirley felt that her time at The Shulamite's House was a refuge from the former storms. God gave her a season of respite.

From the time that Mother Shirley was a young child, there was a call on her life to minister to those in the military. Through the years the young army officer who listened to her radio program kept in touch with Mother Shirley, in time coming to call her mom. One evening he invited a friend of his to a home fellowship so that his friend, a Navel officer could meet his adopted spiritual mother. All evening she had a feeling that somehow she knew him. As he was leaving, she asked if his father was a POW during the Vietnam War. He said, "Yes." It turned out that she wore his father's POW bracelet during the war and prayed for his father everyday during the war. His father was a POW in the Hanoi Hilton for six years. His father almost died as a result of a horrendous one week torture session he had to endure. He was released in 1973, with the other POW's Vietnam returned to the United States. God set the foundation years ago when she wore his father's bracelet paving the way for this young man to also adopt her as his spiritual mother. Today, he is a high ranking Naval Officer.

Mother Shirley's Core Books, Chapters and Verses from the Bible[40]

The Song of Solomon and Malachi are two of Shirley's core books of the Bible. She resonates with the unlovely Shulamite woman rejected by others, but loved by the king. Several of her core chapters are Matthew 6, 7, and 8 and Colossians 3. An important core passage for her is Matthew 6:28-35. She believes that one can live the Christian life with just those books and chapters. The common threads of unconditional love and radical obedience that run through Mother Shirley's life mirror the teachings in her core book and core chapters on love and living righteously. Most of her ministry insights and core values reflect her core book, chapters, and verses.

Each year the sisterhood writes the names of a book from the Bible on a piece of paper and then folds the paper over. Each Sister selected a folded piece of paper with the name of the book written on it. They all made a commitment to read it everyday until it was memorized. The sisters also had to write the book out by longhand. She said that it would be difficult if someone selected a long book to memorize!

---

[39] The Song of Solomon is one of Mother Shirley's major core books in the Bible. A core book is a book that one spends a lot of time studying because of its relevance to the reader. A core book is one that is used repeatedly in ministry as well.

[40] Through Dr. Clinton's research, he discovered that leaders who finish well have what he terms core books, chapters, and verses from the Bible that seem to act as anchor points guiding and shaping the leader's principles and values. Dr. Clinton writes, "Effective leaders should have an appropriate, unique, lifelong plan for mastering the Word to use it with impact in their ministries." He discovered this breakthrough insight of "core" while doing his research. For a more in-depth study of core books, chapters, verses, and topics refer to **Having a Ministry that Lasts**.

D. Mother to the Rejected

(1998- 2002) Age = 65 – 69

Mother Shirley embarked upon a new ministry to the rejected by visiting the female inmates at the Tennessee Women's Prison in 1998. She went there every week holding chapel services and special celebratory services during the holidays. Many of these young female inmates were hard core criminals. There were several known for their violent nature both within and without the prison. Over the course of time she earned the respect of all of the female inmates and of the wardens.

Respect must be earned before one will listen. In a prison system the inmates will not listen to someone they do not respect. Mother Shirley earned their respect by honoring and loving them unconditionally. While ministering to the women inmates, she discovered from personal experience and by watching other Christian groups ministering in the prison that people respond best when they are allowed the freedom to make their own decisions without coercion.

There was one inmate Maxie (not her real name) known for her violence. She was sent to prison for murdering another woman. While in prison, she murdered again, this time an incarcerated woman who had testified against her. This violent inmate had a rosary in her room. She never allowed the Christian groups who ministered in the prison to see her rosary, even though its existence was well known. One day she invited Mother Shirley into her cell where the rosary hung conspicuously on the wall.

Curious, Mother Shirley asked, "Where did you get the rosary?"

"Somebody gave it to me," the Maxie replied.

"Do you say the rosary?" Mother Shirley responded.

"No," Maxie said. "I just like it. It's pretty."

Mother Shirley asked, "Do you know what a rosary is?

This hard-core criminal replied, "Prayers, isn't it."

"Yes. Do you know what kind of prayers?"

"I don't know," she said.

Mother Shirley explained, "In the beginning it was boughs of roses woven into a crown as the person prayed. Just think of taking roses and weaving a crown up in heaven with Jesus."

"Oh" Maxie said. "Would you teach me to say it then?

Pleased, Mother Shirley replied, "Yes, we can say it together."

Other Christian groups tried to reach out to Maxie through a method known as bible-banging. They would quote scripture and tell her how wrong and bad she was. Then they would tell her what she should do but without expressing genuine love and care for her. Mother Shirley watched how this woman distanced herself from those Christian groups, all the while inviting Mother Shirley to spend time with her in her cell.

Mother Shirley's generosity was not limited to love. She always wears a cross. If one of the inmates admired her cross, she quickly took it off and gave it to her without giving it a second thought. She gave many crosses away to the female inmates. At Christmas, Mother Shirley gave each of the female inmates a small plastic baby Jesus as a gift. The inmates walked around carrying that tiny plastic baby Jesus in their hands cradling it as though it were a real baby. The inmates loved Mother Shirley.

During this time she felt like a failure because of a situation arising in the bible study she taught within her community. Some in her bible study wanted to practice the Inward Examination Method. The premise is to seek healing by reflecting on each painful memory, one at a time. Mother Shirley disagreed with this method not because she was against inner healing but because her group had already spent much time seeking inner healing. She felt it unwise to regress instead of going forward. As a result, she was shunned by her community.[41] By going to the prison she was able to focus on the needs of these young women and stop focusing on the most recent rejection by those in her bible study. Several of the Sisters of the Franciscan Order of the Cloistered Heart attended this bible study and quit the sisterhood over this disagreement over the bible study focus. That grieved Mother Shirley deeply. She said that going to the prison and ministering to the female inmates was life-giving to her.

The female inmates were attracted to Mother Shirley. They loved her, because she loved them. The other Christian groups ministering in the prison did not understand how to communicate the message of Christ's love in a loving manner. Mother Shirley discovered while ministering to the women that love is the way. Years prior she prayed and asked God to transform her life so that it mirrored Madame Guyon's life. This was yet another piece of that transformation. Loving others was always difficult for Mother Shirley. It was through this time of ministering to the women that she came to understand what love looked like in action.

She noticed one young woman, Angie (not her real name) who never attended the Bible study. As a child this woman was molested by a grocery man who gave her candy. This woman spent most of her life in prison as a result of murdering two people. She also embraced the homosexual lifestyle. Shirley told the warden that she wanted to meet with Angie. The warden summoned the woman to the chapel so that Mother Shirley could meet with her. In Mother Shirley's words,

> The warden said, "You're on your own. I'll call her down, but you are on your own." I said, "OK." Angie came down and asked the female warden what she wanted. She said, "Sister Shirley wants to see you." She responded, "What did I do?" She came and sat down at the table across from me. I said, "I want to ask you to forgive us as the church for not being there when you needed us." Angie broke down and cried. I said, "I am so sorry. I am so sorry for the pain you had to endure." From then on, she never avoided me. She's out now. She joined the Catholic Church. She has a sponsor from the church and they found a place for her to live.

There are many similar stories like this one where Mother Shirley was able to connect at a heart-level with these female inmates. It was through the following incident that she learned that love is the way to reach people.

The wardens noticed that Maxie, the female inmate who was on death row for butchering her victim while she was still alive always calmed down when she was able to see Mother Shirley. One day while Mother Shirley visited her in her cell she told Mother Shirley,

---

[41] This is a ministry conflict process item. Ministry conflict reflects decisions made by immature emerging leaders. The people in her group were emerging as leaders and in their immaturity made some poor choices by not submitting to their leader (Shirley). Shirley did not force her authority over them, she withdrew. Clinton states that with spiritual authority you cannot force others to submit. Either they do or they don't. If one forces one's personal spiritual authority upon others, it becomes coercive.

If I ever become a Christian, I am going to be just like you, Sister Shirley. I am going to be a Catholic. Mother Shirley responded, "Do you know what a Catholic is Heather (not her real name)? Heather responded in poor English, "You a Catholic aren't you." Answering, Mother Shirley said, "Well I am a Christian first and a Catholic second. You need to be a Christian first and then decide what path (denomination) you are going to follow." Heather responded, "I will be just like you, a Catholic."

Illness initiates a new boundary[42]

Coinciding with the escalating conflict over the Inward Examination Method, Mother Shirley became sick. Holly was concerned. Her mother's illness triggered another thought. Her parents lived so far away. What would happen if her father became ill without anyone there to help Mother Shirley care for him? Through that painful conflict with the small group, God initiated the beginning of a boundary through Holly's invitation for her parents to move to Tennessee. Holly and her second husband owned ten acres. Holly told her mother that she could pick any location on their property to live. Holly's invitation was appealing as it coincided with Shirley's community kicking her out because she would not embrace the Inward Examination. Many of her spiritual children who lived in other states did not understand why she and Pop decided to make the move to Tennessee. From their perspective her decision to move was a mistake as they were unaware that Shirley's community had shunned her because of the conflict. What she did not know was that God used her illness to transition her into convergence.[43]

Ministry Insights for PHASE IV

a. The Broad Umbrella

The "broad umbrella" concept that Mother Shirley gleaned while she and Bill attended the Keswick conferences was foundational in how she structured the Franciscan Order of the Cloistered Heart Sisterhood. Women of any denomination could join[44]. She did not require non-Catholics to renounce their Protestant heritage in order to become a sister.

Mother Shirley also uses the concept of the "broad umbrella" as a foundation for structuring her spiritual retreats. She welcomes all who are spiritually hungry regardless of their denominational allegiance. At her retreats it is common to see Catholics, Orthodox, Protestants and Charismatics all worshipping together showing incredible respect and honor toward one another. For example, at one recent spiritual retreat several of the Sisters were ordained as deacons in the Syrian Orthodox Church. The priest officiated the ceremony, shortened it from the normal hour down to thirty minutes because he knew that the Protestants in attendance would find it hard to stay engaged since they are not accustomed to long liturgies.

---

[42] Each personal time-line is divided into PHASES demarcating different time periods in a person's life. Each PHASE is then divided further into sub-phases of smaller segments. A boundary is a series of incidences which transition an individual from one major life PHASE to another major life PHASE.

[43] "It refers to the fifth development PHASE of the generalized time-line." (Clinton 1988:238) In this PHASE the leader's gift-mix, experience, spiritual authority etc. are all matched. Everything converges together resulting in fruit in ministry.

[44] Fifteen years after establishing the order, the first brother was admitted.

b. Obedience Can Be Threatening

Obedience can threaten immature leaders. Immature leaders use their authority incorrectly by coercing or manipulating their followers into following. Those who have spiritual authority do not coerce or manipulate. Mother Shirley gained a ministry insight from her historical mentor, Madame Guyon. When she was denounced by the charismatic pastors she learned that "suffering is the only means to get to the glory." God often uses negative circumstances to refine us, to open up new growth opportunities, and to increase our spiritual authority. Her right response to this negative process item prepared her to handle increased spiritual authority and influence.

c. You can't make decisions for others!

As Mother Shirley reflected upon the situation where Angie asked her the question about homosexuality and other incidences with the female inmates, she realized that she could not make decisions for other people. When she presents Christ to people, her presentation must be done so that people have a choice. This experience forged the value that one cannot make decisions for other people.

Strategic Development from PHASE IV

Shirley grew into the mother God intended her to be according to the prophetic word given to her some years prior that she would be a "Mother of Israel with hundreds, yea thousands of children." Her heart for the abused increased substantially when she took in her two grandsons and daughter after her son-in-law almost killed the oldest grandson. It appeared from Shirley's development over the years that God allowed her to experience the pain of the people to whom she was called to minister. She knew first hand how it felt to be an emotional orphan, how it felt to see your loved-one almost killed through a fit of rage, and how those abandoned by others felt. A common destiny theme seems to be a calling to those abandoned by others. This theme is what shaped her as a spiritual mother. In this PHASE God prepared her by allowing her to experience the hopelessness of abandonment and the pain of rejection so that she could empathize with her spiritual children. These extreme experiences prepare her for the next PHASE where she will begin walking in the greatest gift she could give to any child, that of love.

BIOGRAPHICAL PHASE V: No Cost Too Great

(2002 to the present) Age = 69 to the present

A. Healing Touch

(2002-2006) Age = 69 – 74

It was hard being kicked out of yet another group over focus of ministry. Mother Shirley left North Carolina dejected. She lost that ministry and all of her friends who lived in that community. When she moved to Sparta, Tennessee in 2002 she entered the dark night of her soul.[45] She had no ministry, no friends, and no church. She felt like a failure. Adding to this weight of failure, Pop discovered two weeks after he retired that his retirement fund had been embezzled and they were left without any retirement. Within a week he went back to work for the same company he worked at prior. He never once complained about the injustice of this loss. They also discovered that Social Security was not enough for them to live on. Without the retirement income, it was necessary for him to go back to work. His only comment made the next morning after this revelation was, "I guess it was not in God's plan for us to retire." He is in his seventies and plans to work until his health forces him to cease working.

During this first year in Sparta, Tennessee, Mother Shirley attended the Catholic Church about two times. She had no desire to connect with people. She wanted to build a small prayer closet next to where she and Pop located their trailer on Holly's property. Pop encouraged her to expand her prayer closet from the actual size of a clothes closet to the size of a room. She complied with his wishes not understanding why she would need a large chapel. During this time she even stopped hosting her fall spiritual retreats, as she considered herself a failure. It was during this time that God began a profound work of grace in her life. It happened gradually. When she and Pop moved to Sparta, she had to discontinue going to the women's prison as the drive was too far for her. However, the lessons learned there about how to love people began to flourish in her life.

Mother Shirley practices "as you go ministry." Wherever she goes, she ministers. For example, she is a connoisseur of fine food. She found a restaurant and began to frequent it every week. She loved on the waitresses leaving them generous tips of twenty or thirty per-cent of the total food bill. She took an interest in their lives and mothered them. In time, the waitresses and waiters asked her to teach a bible study. Next they asked where she went to church. She told them that she did not go to church but that she had a prayer chapel on her property next to her trailer. They were welcome to attend on Sunday morning if they desired. Most of the waitresses and waiters were people who either did not know the Lord or who had been hurt by the church and as a result no longer went to church.

---

[45] This reference comes from a book written by Brother Lawrence called **The Dark Night of the Soul**. The term refers to that season in one's life in which the person feels that all has been stripped away and God is silent. It is interesting to observe the timing of Shirley's personal dark night of the soul. It happened just before she entered convergence. See footnote 42, for definition of convergence. Also, after she emerged from this season she began practicing the manifest and the unbiased love for others at a new depth and with greater intensity than ever before.

However, Shirley never intended to start a church. Every morning at 8 a.m. Charlene a faithful Sister of the order would come and the two of them would pray, even on Sundays. Soon, her daughter Holly asked if she could join them for prayer on Sunday mornings. Next, Mother Shirley's house keeper wanted to join them. Now it was Pop, Mother Shirley, Charlene, Holly, and the housekeeper. Soon, the waitresses and the waiters wanted to start attending. The prayer meeting morphed into a church service.

People were attracted to how she loves. She loved and allowed the Holy Spirit to convict of sin. Many of the people drawn to her struggled with moral issues. She taught God's word with power and allowed the Holy Spirit to literally convict them of those areas in their lives that needed changing. The result was that the people conformed to the prompting of the Holy Spirit and not to the rules set by man.

Two young waitresses were attracted to Mother Shirley. Ellen (not her real name), one of the young women invited Abby (not her real name) to attend the Bible study at Mother Shirley's place on Monday nights. For awhile Abby blew Ellen off refusing to attend. Finally she relented and came. This is what she said,

> I really needed someone to lead me in the right way. Amber and the others were coming up here for awhile and I had known them for the past years. Their lives had changed dramatically since I had known them. I blew Ellen off a couple of times. I don't think I wanted to go up there. Finally, I came up here and I am so glad I did. There was a group of us that came that night. I just felt like she (Mother Shirley) was speaking straight to my heart – she knew everything that was going on and I got up and hugged her and the second I hugged her, I started bawling. And I was embarrassed that I was losing it. When I hugged her I felt – you feel something holy – you know – you just feel it. It is the most pure love. It's just amazing. The second I touched her I broke down and bawled. I've been up here ever since – every Monday. I haven't missed a Monday. I've been here every Sunday. And I love it. I love being up here. And everybody that comes up here is like – I don't know, it's like the strongest family bond that you have in your own family.[46]

Both Ellen and Abby were involved in relationships outside of marriage. Mother Shirley never spoke to them about those relationships, instead she allowed the Holy Spirit to conviction. After they accepted Christ, God supernaturally intervened and separated them out of the relationships. It was painful for the both of them as they had to grieve the emotional loss. Soon after conversion they decided that their clothes were no longer appropriate and that they needed to slowly buy a new wardrobe. This decision was based on the conviction of the Holy Spirit in their lives and not due to anything that Mother Shirley spoke to them because she said nothing to them about how they dressed. One of the young women has since joined the Sisterhood. The other entered into Officer Candidate School for the military.

A few years later, she started helping out at a Syrian Orthodox church in Knoxville that has a street ministry to the street people. She would cook and take meals to them once a week or every other week. The people who attend are street people. Mother Shirley was impressed by how these holy men loved the street people. In time, she and her sisters changed their order from being Catholic to being aligned with the Syrian Orthodox church. They changed the name to The Order of the Myrrhbearers.

---

[46] This quote was taken from an interview with Abby at Mother Shirley's home in June, 2006.

She was invited to attend Diaconate School so that she could be ordained as a deacon in the Syrian Orthodox Church. She was the only woman in the class with learned men fluent in several ancient languages. They treated her with great respect by calling her "amma," which is Greek for mother.

During this time, Shirley also became a master teacher teaching icon classes in the Tennessee area. Once she took an old satellite dish and painted an icon of Jesus on it and then she placed the painting in the ceiling of her chapel. She paints and gives the icon paintings away as gifts to her spiritual children.

She also resumed her spiritual retreats with the sisters in her sisterhood. The sisters prepare for the spiritual retreat for approximately six months out of the year. They pray and ask God for the theme each year. Then they spend time preparing "words" for each attendant. They choreograph dances for the times of worship with a team of dancers. Mother Shirley no longer has the dance troupes like she once did, but some of the original dancers belong to the Sisterhood. Often during the worship while people are watching the dancers dance before the Lord, someone will break down emotionally, weeping before the Lord receiving deep healing without one word being spoken. When that happens, others will come along side and minister. The people who attend her conferences love her deeply.

Often people who are legalistic seem to react to Mother Shirley's presence. It could be that they view her gray habit as a Catholic threat. Once, while she was eating at a restaurant a young man approached her table. He hit the table with his fist and threw his hands into the air next to Mother Shirley's and Sister Charlene's faces. "I want to know something," he said, "Is Jesus Christ the center of your religion?" Mother Shirley responded, "No sir, He is not. He is the center of my life. I do not have religion." He glowered at them, turned around and went back to his table.

Another time a young man walked up to Mother Shirley's table at a restaurant and demanded to know which version of the Bible she read. She said that she read several different versions of the Bible. He then proceeded to inform her that only the King James Version was acceptable. To that she replied that any version was better than watching TV. At this response, he got up and quickly left her table.

B. The Order of the Myrrhbearers Grows

(2006 -) Age = 73 on
Afterglow[47]

For many years the Sisterhood remained steady in numbers. After the bible study in North Carolina shunned Mother Shirley in 2002, she lost several sisters. In 2006, the sisterhood started growing with the induction of a young woman who was a waitress. In 2007, the Sisterhood inducted new sisters and their first "brother" into the Order.

God is honoring Mother Shirley for her faithfulness to him all of these years. The Syrian Orthodox Church is preparing to ordain her and her friend Jackie into the priesthood in the fall of 2008. They are taking classes to prepare for the ordination.

---

[47] Afterglow refers to the fallout effect of a life well-lived. In this phase spiritual authority is dominant. This is certainly true in Mother Shirley's life at this time.

Since 2006, her fall spiritual retreats reflect the "broad umbrella" approach with the Syrian Orthodox priests attending along side of the Catholics, Protestants, and Charismatics. The spiritual retreats reflect how she models love. In order to keep the Sisterhood going after her death, the Sisters decided how to ensure the continuance of leadership.

In this time of afterglow, people come from many states just to be in Mother Shirley's presence. Every week she has guests that come from great distances just to spend time in her presence. Not long ago a woman asked if she could come and spend a few days with Mother Shirley. She drove from Wisconsin to Tennessee. At the end of the three days, Mother Shirley asked her if she received what she needed. "Oh, yes," she replied. "Now I feel peaceful." This always amazes Mother Shirley. From Mother Shirley's perspective all she does is listen to the people who come and feed them. She says, "God does the rest."

Ministry Insights for PHASE V

a. Love is the way

When she ministered at the prison, Mother Shirley discovered the ministry insight of "my job is to love them, its God's job to straighten them out." This perspective opened the door for her to love at the same depth as her historical mentor, Madame Guyon. She used this ministry insight one time with a young woman involved with a married man who claimed to be a Christian. The young woman had just accepted Christ as her Savior. Upset over how this married man was using the young woman, Mother Shirley wanted to tell him how he was hurting both his wife and this young woman. However, Mother Shirley did not. Because of this principle she actually relied on the Holy Spirit to convict the young woman that her affair was wrong. Mother Shirley said nothing to her about her affair even though she had just accepted Christ. In anger one day, Mother Shirley told the Lord what she wanted to say to the married man. She felt that the Holy Spirit impressed upon her that He would speak her thoughts directly into his heart. Two weeks later, the young woman came to Mother Shirley in tears telling her what the married man told her, that he was ruining her life and hurting his wife by having the affair. He broke it off. Then the Holy Spirit also revealed to the young woman that her affair was wrong.

Her ministry insight of "it's my job is to love them, its God's job to straighten them out" actually forces her spiritual children to learn how to depend upon the Lord instead of depending upon her for guidance. She loves and teaches God's truth, the Holy Spirit convicts, and they learn how to respond to the voice of the Lord. The net result is that when the Holy Spirit convicts of sinful choices or lifestyle habits the conviction is between them and the Lord and not between them and Mother Shirley. She does not play Holy Spirit in their life. This is what makes her so appealing to many people.

b. Be Prepared!

One time the Lord prompted Mother Shirley to give a token of love to a woman sitting at a booth in the restaurant in which she was eating. It is Mother Shirley's custom to always carry with her some token of God's love that she can give away in a moment's notice. Today, she had nothing except a small booklet written by Mother Basilea.

Shirley motioned to the waitress and asked if she would give the woman the little book after she left the restaurant. She slipped her card into the booklet. Six years later, this woman wrote Mother Shirley a note and mailed it to her. She explained that on the day the waitress gave her Mother Shirley's booklet, she was considering embracing new age teachings and beliefs. She did not because she read Mother Basilea's booklet. Instead she made a decision for Christ.

Spiritual Development from PHASE V

There is a saying that the fiercest fighting happens just before breakthrough. For Shirley, this happened at the conclusion of PHASE IV. From her perspective she lost everything, her ministries, her friends, and her home. The Inward Focus Method ministry conflict brought her into the dark night of her soul, a time when she could not see what God was doing. One of Mother Shirley's favorite sayings is "What man takes away, God supplies." God was getting ready to bring into fulfillment the prayer she prayed years ago to make her like Madame Guyon. Out of the ashes of what she perceived was her end arose an understanding of manifest and unbiased love. As she began to walk in this new understanding of love she unexpectedly entered into convergence. Convergence is a state where the ministry location, the well-developed spiritual gifts, one's experience, the spiritual authority one has, and the sphere of influence all converge allowing her to become the spiritual mother God called her to be.

CRITICAL INCIDENTS

A critical incident is a shaping activity God uses to forge a major value or to impart strategic direction in the life of the leader. The cumulative impact of the critical incidences over a period of time in the life of the leader shapes "all three types of formations – spiritual (leadership character), ministerial (leadership skills), and strategic (total direction in life and ministry, leadership vision)" (Clinton 1995:103).

Shirley selected the following incidents that she felt forged her spiritual, ministerial and strategic values as a leader.

Incident Name	Age	Formational Type – Basic Value
1. The Candy Bars	7-8	**Spiritual & Ministerial:** When Shirley was 7 years old, she was sent to live with her relatives when her mother had a nervous breakdown after the divorce. Her relatives did not want her. They placed a bed for her in the living room dishonoring her presence by not giving her a separate room, as was the custom in American culture. In the evening, while Shirley was in bed, but not asleep, her aunt and uncle would sit in the living room and eat candy and drink soda in front of her without ever offering her any. This repeated incident ***formed a spiritual value*** that one ought always to share with all who are present. This value shaped her later ministry of always giving gifts to all who attend her spiritual retreats, her teas, or any other event she hosts.
2. Military Hymns	9	**Strategic:** Every morning while Shirley was in the fourth grade, the teacher began the morning session by having the class sing military hymns. The singing of the hymns caused Shirley to disrupt the class through her wailing, as she could not sing without crying. The teacher made her stand outside of the classroom where she could weep without disrupting the others. This was an ***early shaping incident*** revealing a future call of the Lord to Shirley to minister to those serving in the military.
3. Salvation	33	**Personal & Strategic:** In this personal and strategic incident Shirley experienced a profound and life shattering paradigm shift when she accepted Christ as her savior. Before her salvation all she experienced was the lack of faithfulness on the part of those who professed to love. She accepted Christ when she heard that he was faithful. In that moment she made the decision to learn everything about this man and do whatever he wanted. That ***decision became a key focal value***[48] that no cost would be too great in obeying Jesus.

[48] Dr. Clinton defines a focal value as "a dominant controlling perspective (a leadership value), which interweaves itself throughout a person's ministry and usually can be traced to a critical incident." (Clinton 1995a:19) Her decision that night to find out about this man (Jesus) and do whatever he wanted became a key focal value that no cost would be too great in obeying Jesus became the critical incident. As one traces her life, it is apparent that she was willing to pay the steep personal cost of following Jesus. She did so with an ever-increasing measure of grace.

4. Keswick Conferences	33-43	**Spiritual:** During a period of ten years, Shirley and her husband attended the summer Keswick conferences in Ashville, North Carolina. These conferences came out of the Keswick Movement from Capernwray, England. She met and then became an acquaintance of Robert McQuilkin, son of the founder of Colombia Bible College. Robert McQuilkin embraced the "broad umbrella" perspective of including many evangelical streams. The "broad umbrella" term ***became a foundational perspective*** directing Shirley to steer away from strong denominationalism that was prevalent at that time and embrace ecumenicalism in her approach to ministry. A second shaping incident happened when Shirley witnessed McQuilkin tell Dr. Van Gorder that he would not be able to teach on "charismatic confusion" or offer his books for sale on that subject. McQuilkin told him that the Keswick Conference was a "broad umbrella" and if he could not speak on another topic, he could not speak. Shirley observed that Dr. Van Gorder never complained and that he did what was asked and spoke on a different topic. From that incident she ***learned how to submit to those in authority with right attitudes***. God would use this shaping incident to forge a set of values and principles that later guarded her heart when she was unjustly treated by men in leadership.
5. "Half-time"	36	**Ministerial:** In 1969, while Shirley watched a football game with her children, a ***ministerial value of celebration*** formed during the half-time show. She witnessed the splendor of the half-time celebration and decided that the Church needed to celebrate Jesus like the football fans celebrate football. This insight prompted her to form a dance troupe, a tambourine team, and a sword team to celebrate the Lord's presence. In a short time, ***these processionals became an effective methodology.***
6. POW/MIA Bracelet	36	**Strategic:** Shirley's small community ordered some POW/MIA bracelets for a military personnel captured or lost during the Vietnam War. This critical incident laid the foundation for a future meeting with the son of the captured pilot. Today the son is a high ranking naval officer. He too, calls Shirley "mom."
7. Honor Others	37	**Strategic:** Shirley was invited to host a celebration processional featuring dance and music for Gwen Shaw and her ministry. Prior to the event, while in preparation, the Lord impressed upon Shirley the need to honor Gwen and her husband during the event. Unknown to Shirley, Gwen had suffered some difficult situations that left her wounded. Shirley witnessed the powerful effect honor had on this leader and how it brought healing. She decided then that she would always honor someone at her retreats. From then on the ***value of honoring others became foundational*** to how she ministered to others.
8. My Sin Hurts Others	41	**Spiritual:** Eight years after Shirley became a Christian, she still smoked cigarettes. She tried to stop numerous times without success. She finally told God that she tried but that she just couldn't stop. A short time later her daughter Holly was riding a horse when the horse tripped

		and fell on top of her. Holly was rushed to the hospital in critical condition. While Shirley sat in the hallway, she sensed the Lord say, "You've told me that you can't quit smoking. Now I've touched something that you do love. Lay them (the cigarettes) down and I will raise her up." Stunned, Shirley was faced with the consequences of her own sin afflicting the life of someone close to her. From this critical incident she learned a ***strategic insight*** that sin can often affect the ones we love in negative ways. From this she learned the ***value that leaders ought never to tell God that the cost is too great to depend upon Him. God will either give the leader the opportunity to depend upon Him or if the leader refuses to repent, provide more opportunities to learn how to depend upon God.***
9. Mother Basilea	43	**Spiritual and Strategic:** Mother Basilea was a divine contact and contemporary mentor for Shirley. Shirley was ready to give up on the Church and was desperate to find a Christian leader who actually practiced what the scriptures taught. An Episcopalian minister listened to Shirley share and recommended the books written by Mother Basilea, a Lutheran woman who founded the Canaan of the Desert Order. ***Her writings shaped Shirley's ministry philosophy and her value system***. She was a ***contemporary mentor*** to Shirley.
10. Living in Community	44	**Spiritual & Ministerial:** Going into community was accidental. Frank and Jackie wanted to live closer to Shirley and Bill so that they could attend their home group. Frank and Jackie sold their house but could not find anything for sale in the same small town where Shirley and Bill lived. The Raper's invited Frank and Jackie to move in with them for a couple of months until they could find their own place. Within a matter of weeks, nineteen people moved into a one bathroom house. This happened right after Shirley was kicked out of the baptist church when her ***paradigm shifted from viewing the Church as a building to viewing it as the Body of Believers.***
11. Purged	45	**Personal:** A few years after Shirley accepted the Lord she continued to struggle with rejection. One day she was so disgusted with her state of being that she said to two friends, "I want to walk through my life, I want to be done with these things. I want you all to help me." That night Mother Shirley's two friends spent three hours in prayer ministering to her. At the end of that time Mother Shirley experienced complete healing from the feelings of inferiority and superiority. This spiritual victory was strategic because most of the people she is called to minister to suffer from feelings of inferiority. ***In order for her to minister effectively***, she had to experience profound healing.
12. Heart Attack	47	**Spiritual:** In 1980 Shirley suffered a heart attack. When she was taken to the hospital she panicked because she could not sense the Lord. Looking at the crucifix on the wall, she prayed and asked God, "Where were you? I couldn't find you. You said that you would never leave me." The Lord's reply accompanied the mental picture of seeing a finger dipped in a cup of water and touching

		Shirley's tongue, "Ere a baby too young to drink, his mother wets his tongue with a drop, so have I let you taste of what it was like when I turned my face from Jesus when he took your sins." Shirley later said that experienced provided a ***pivotal understanding*** that suffering received correctly causes us to love God more. This understanding was strategic because Shirley suffered much dishonor from other Christians. It helped her persevere through the difficult times.
13. Abandoned	58	**Strategic:** Shirley was awakened at 2 a.m. in the morning with an overwhelming feeling of abandonment and hopelessness. This happened again the next night. She asked the Lord, "Lord, what is wrong with me to feel this way?" Then she saw a picture of men in cages with a man standing guard outside of the cages with a gun. She said, "Lord, I don't understand what I am seeing." The Lord told her, "It is the men your nation left behind." She called a friend who was former military. He explained that what she saw was a North Vietnamese prison compound. This experienced was strategic in praying for the living POW's the United States left behind after the Vietnam War ended. The POW/MIAs ***became a prayer focus*** for many years.
14. Mar Michael	71	**Strategic:** Mar Michael is an ordained priest in the Syrian Orthodox Church. Shirley met him in 2002. ***This divine contact became a mentor sponsoring Shirley into higher ranks of leadership within the Syrian Orthodox Church increasing her sphere of influence***. She will be ordained a priest in the fall of 2008. This critical incident is the culmination of the previous critical incidents and her right attitudes to all of the painful shaping experiences God used to test her.

Most of Mother Shirley's critical incidents seem to be strategic or spiritual in nature. She learned her values from her historical mentor, Madame Guyon, from her contemporary mentor, Mother Basilea, and from her life-long mentor, Sister Lucia. Her values and her natural talents shaped her ministry. She is a visionary leader. Early in her ministry she caught a vision of celebrating the majesty of God through processional. She was able to take that vision and translate it into actual ministry.

Several other insights drawn from these critical incidents:

1. **God prepares us even when we are not aware.**

As a child, Shirley was not thinking about her destiny. Her focus was on the present and not on the future. Yet, God used her present circumstances to prepare her for the future. The candy bar incident formed within her the importance of being generous to all present. God redeemed the pain she experienced as a child in isolation by bringing healing to many later in life when she was an adult.

2. **Spiritual authority is a by-product of focusing on the Lord.**

Shirley never sought spiritual authority. It increased as she consistently obeyed the Lord.

3. **God custom tailors critical incidents to fit one's ultimate contributions[49] and one's giftedness set.**

This insight allows the recipient to experience a child-like trust and confidence in what God is doing. That perspective should cause the recipient to focus their attention on what God is working out through the difficult or painful circumstance with the idea that ultimately something good will result. This insight enables the recipient to experience a critical incident with a full expectation that God is in control and that the critical incident will contribute to the person's destiny. This posture allows for quick forgiveness, protects against bitterness, and prevents competition and jealousy from forming against those who seem to enjoy wonderful critical incidences.

VALUES

Listed here are some of the most important values that guided and shaped Mother Shirley's life. These values developed over the course of her life. Some of the values she adopted from her historical mentor, Madame Guyon, while other values came from her contemporary mentor, Mother Basilea. She discovered many of her values from critical incidents or through positive and negative processing items. By each listed value an illustrative example shows how that value directed her actions. Some of the values run like a thread throughout her life. In addition to the illustrative examples, if the value was adopted from one of her mentors, it is noted which mentor imparted the value. This notation occurs so that the development of that particular value can be traced.

1. **People should be honored.**
   This story is listed in the Critical Incident Chart. When Shirley observed the healing affect honor had on the recipient, she decided to make honoring people foundational to her ministry. At every spiritual retreat she hosts, people are honored by the giving of gifts, ministry, and through personal blessing.

2. **A leader ought to glean wherever he or she goes.**
   This value was adopted by Mother Shirley from her historical mentor, Madame Guyon. She taught that one must always glean something positive from every situation. Madame Guyon's perspective was that since all things must pass through the hand of God before coming to an individual, it is imperative to accept all as from the hand of God and not to complain. This value protected Mother Shirley from nurturing bitterness when she was kicked out of the various denominations.

[49] For a detailed explanation of an ultimate contribution, turn to page 51 of **Strategic Concepts that Clarify A Focused Life**.

3. **Victory/success should be measured not by the abundance or lack of material possessions, but by having the right attitude!**
   Mother Shirley can honestly say that material things do not mean anything to her. If a guest mentions that he or she admires something in her home, she is quick to give the object to the admirer. Some people seek poverty as a means to living a victorious Christian life, however, Mother Shirley counters this practice by stating that the victory is not whether or not one has or does not have possessions; victory resides within the desires of the heart. She says, "Not having anything is not victory. Not wanting anything is victory."

4. **A leader should embrace one's cross in its various forms, as well as any accompanying pain!**
   "Circumstances are designed by God – always! Satan may be the errand boy, but God made him do it. When circumstances come in the form of a cross or pain, embrace it! This side is black and dark. The other side is pure gold."[50] This value reflects the teaching of both Madame Guyon and Mother Basilea. Mother Shirley embraces the cross and the pain of any situation by responding in a non-defensive manner. She allows God to be her defense. If God should chose not to defend her, then she will not defend herself to those attacking her.

5. **There are no losses in God.**
   Mother Shirley believes that when someone experiences a loss, God will have something better. When she was kicked out of the baptist church, she and Pop started attending a church which believed in and practiced all of the spiritual gifts. They also participated in a home group in which they witnessed healings and miracles. Had they stayed at the baptist church, this may not have happened. Sometimes God allows a loss in order to give us something better. This value and paradigm was adopted from Madame Guyon's teachings.

6. **A leader should value legitimate suffering from God.**
   This reflects Madame Guyon's teaching. During an interview in which Mother Shirley was asked about her view on suffering, she said, "It is not the end; it is the means to get you to the glory. Yes, you will suffer. You can make it count for good or you can be miserable. You take your choice! Everything we have is a choice. If you make him (Jesus) your everything, I can assure you that everything else will fall into place."[51]

7. **A leader must not make decisions for other people.**
   Shirley learned this value while ministering to the female inmates that the Tennessee Women's Prison. The answer given to "Angie," the female inmate, who asked the question about homosexuality, gave rise to the value that no one can make decisions for other people. This value shaped how Mother Shirley discipled new Christians. She taught them about the Lord using scripture. She did not instruct new Christians telling them that they have to stop smoking or stop

---

[50] This quote was taken from Mother Shirley during an interview with in Tennessee, June 2006
[51] Ibid.

living immoral lives. One time a gentleman she knew wanted to attend her fall retreat with his mistress. He wanted to meet with Mother Shirley to talk about the possibility of attending. She met them (the man and his mistress) at the hotel and told him that he had some decisions to make. Point blank she explained how he dishonored both his wife and his mistress by living the life he was living and that he needed to make a decision. He claimed to be a Christian. She never told him that he should reconcile with his wife and leave his mistress. Instead since she embraces the value that she cannot make decisions for others, she left after she explained clearly how his actions were hurting the very people he claimed to love. The decision was his alone to make. He did not to attend the fall retreat that year.

8. **A leader ought to honor the name of the Lord!**
   Honoring the Lord is foundational to all Mother Shirley does. She believes that we honor or dishonor the name of the Lord by how we live, in addition to how one speaks. Because she is a connoisseur of fine food she eats out often. She said, "If you can afford to eat out but not tip, then stay home and eat a sandwich, but do not bring shame on the name of the Lord by not tipping or leaving a small tip." The reason why she has so much success in sharing Christ with waitresses and waiters is that she honors God through her generosity in tipping. She also incorporates the concept and practice of honor into her spiritual retreats by formally honoring those as directed by God.

9. **When depressed, one ought to praise God!**
   "I tell you how to get out of the hole – sing praises at the top of your lungs."[52] Many times when Bill traveled and Shirley was sick and depressed, alone at home in the middle of the night, she would get out of bed and begin to praise God at the top of her lungs. She would march around the kitchen table singing Christian music to conquer her depression. She marched until the depression lifted, then she would crawl back into bed and fall asleep.

10. **A leader must be generous.**
    When Shirley was a new Christian she had no experience in distinguishing between good and bad Christian leaders. They all sounded good to her. She prayed and asked God to show her how to distinguish between the good and bad Christian leaders. The Lord told her, "When people or leaders don't give, don't follow them. You don't need to judge them, but don't follow them." Generosity is an important value that guides and shapes her life. From tipping at the restaurant to lavishing many gifts upon those who attend her spiritual retreats to generously giving of her time to the many travelers who seek her out, she models generosity.

11. **A leader ought to submit to God.**
    "You have no rights of your own; you don't decide one thing about where you serve." Shirley is adamant that we are to serve where the Lord tells us to serve. If

---

[52] Ibid.

the Lord places one in a difficult situation, that person should stay there until the Lord brings about a release. This value also reflects Madame Guyon's teaching.

12. **Leaders must be available – The availability factor.**
This value under girds her hospitality as she constantly has a stream of visitors coming to stay with her seeking spiritual refreshment. The availability factor refers to the posture of being available when someone has the need and not put the person off until it is convenient.

13. **A leader ought to interpret culture in light of God's Word and not God's Word in light of culture.**
This value allowed Mother Shirley the freedom to practice obedience to God regardless of the cost to her. She said, "I choose to believe God above myself or anyone else."

14. **A leader ought to live in the state of celebration before the Lord!**
This value was birthed when Shirley watched the football game with her children in 1969. As she watched the half-time celebration for the game, she immediately desired to see people celebrate the Lord in the same manner. She views the celebratory nature of her spiritual retreats and the processionals as a covenant renewal time for believers.

15. **A leader ought to pray for those he or she leads.**
Prayer is a habit that Mother Shirley cultivated from the time she was a child. Every morning at 8 a.m. she spends one hour in concentrated prayer. She prays throughout the day. (She has a calendar with the names of those she is called to pray.) Some names are on the calendar everyday for daily intercession.

MINISTRY INSIGHTS, LESSONS, & GENERAL VALUES

Focal Values & Lessons from Mother Shirley's Ministry

There are three major components of Mother Shirley's ministry which need to be examined more closely: **healing, unbiased loved to the Church**, and **manifested love to the lost.**[53] Mother Shirley said that these three values under-gird her motivations, her spiritual gifts, and they are the building blocks for her effective methodologies.

It is interesting to note that two of the three focal values Mother Shirley embraces are the same focal values of her historical mentor, Madame Guyon and her contemporary mentor, Mother Basilea; that of unbiased loved for the church and manifested love to the

[53] It is important to make the distinction between manifest and unbiased love. Manifest means apparent, what is easy to see according to Webster's Dictionary. Unbiased means to be without bias or prejudice. Mother Shirley loves lavishly and does not hide her love for the lost by showing them respect through an absence of fear of association and by being generous in how she interacts with them.

lost. The third focal value, healing is where Mother Shirley diverges from her mentors. These three principles shape how Mother Shirley approaches life and ministry more than all of her other gifts. Mother Shirley is an amazing woman who knows how to love the ones, other Christians shun. Examples are given to illustrate how these three principles operate in her life.

Manifested Love to the Lost:

Mother Shirley knows how to love unconditionally those outside of the Church. She looks like a grandmother who is fun to be around. She is humorous and she knows how to put those who do not know Christ at ease. She exudes love. Her value of expressing manifested love to those outside of the Church causes her to seek out establishments other Christians might shun.

She heard about a floral shop owned by two homosexuals. Other Christians refuse to frequent that shop because of the owners' lifestyle choice. Mother Shirley views the shop as an opportunity to share the love of Christ with the owners; she also likes their floral selections. The gray habit is often an excellent ice breaker causing people to ask Mother Shirley spiritual questions. The owners of the shop noticed her habit and asked what kind of church she attended. She told them that she attended a church in which everybody was welcomed. She was able to make that comment because she meant it. If they decided to attend her church, she would welcome them. That comment opened their hearts to her.

The day prior to Valentine's Day Mother Shirley went to their floral shop to purchase a dozen roses. When she walked in, one of the owners ushered her into the back room so that she could greet the other owner and the workers preparing the flowers. They were excited to see her. They waited on her personally bumping her to the front of a long line, giving her the cash price when she paid with her credit card.

How does she do it? She does not preach at them. She exudes love. As stated previously in a quote by Sarah, "there is something about Mother Shirley when you are in her presence - you sense love."

One time when Mother Shirley was having lunch at a restaurant, a waitress slipped her a note. She wanted Mother Shirley to pray for her as she was a single mom with challenges. This waitress was not a Christian, yet she knew about Mother Shirley's reputation. All during lunch Mother Shirley silently prayed and asked God what needed to be done. Before lunch was over, the group accompanying Mother Shirley collected $93 to give to this single mom. She broke down in tears and hugged Mother Shirley for the longest time.

Every Friday, the wounded soldiers recovering at Walter Reed Hospital are given a hero's welcome tour of the Pentagon. Once, when Mother Shirley happened to be there visiting someone she knew, the tour with the wounded soldiers took place. Mother Shirley just happened to be standing in the hallway with her escort when the tour came by. Many wives and mothers of the soldiers stopped to greet Mother Shirley as they walked down the hallway. An Army General observed the many people who hugged her and requested to meet her. After the meeting the General asked if Mother Shirley would pray for her on a regular basis. Wherever she goes, people are attracted to her.

When she visited the prison there was one violent prisoner on death row who lived in an agitated state. Whenever Mother Shirley came to see her she could calm down. The warden loved it when Mother Shirley came because of her calming effect on the female inmates. The few female prisoners who would not have anything to do with the other Christian groups ministering there would be willing to meet with Mother Shirley.

Where other Christians might be tempted to judge and not feel compassion because of fear that the person might be working the system, or fear of supporting someone involved in an alterative lifestyle, Mother Shirley willingly loves those others quickly reject. Yet her manifest love for the lost does not mean that she has no Christian standards. She accepts all wherever they are. She believes that if a person desires to pursue God without changing, God will remove that person from the influence of her life. She literally leaves that decision in God's hands. If a person never pursues God, she will love that person unconditionally. She makes a distinction between those who desire God without changing and those who are not seeking God at all. That is in keeping with her quote taken from "God's Job" principle, "It is my job to love and it is God's job to straighten the person out."

The bottom line determines one's behavior. Mother Shirley's bottom line is the manifest love of Christ to those who do not know God. That means that she will shop places where others would not shop. She will laugh, joke and pray for those others consider hopeless cases. She mixes respect into her manifest love. The homosexuals who own the florist shop she frequents feel her respect and they love her. When she apologized to the lesbian inmate for the pain and suffering she endured as a child through the act of molestation, she validated that woman's pain which was an act of manifest love. She has an aura about her in which emotional orphans sense love even without her saying anything.

Unbiased Love to the Church:

This focal value of extending unbiased love to those within the Church and those marginalized by the Church shapes how she approaches ministry. Learning how to love those in the Church with an unbiased love has been a difficult road for Shirley. Today, when sitting in her presence it appears that loves comes naturally and easy for her. However, that was not always the case. I asked if I could read her journals in order to learn more about how she loves others. She told me that she is in the process of destroying her journals because when she was a new Christian she did not know how to love and that lack was reflected in her journal entries. Today her love is so strong that it is more important to her to destroy her journals than to let someone be destroyed by an unkind comment she wrote years ago before she knew how to love.

This focal value came from the teachings of Mother Basilea and Madame Guyon. The ice cream parlor analogy best illustrates the value of unbiased love. One day Mother Shirley asked Sister Lucia, how it was possible to work with and love different and difficult people. How can one extend unbiased love toward those who feel adamant about issues for which others do not feel adamant? Sister Lucia gave the classic answer about not having to like or criticize the flavor of ice cream someone else selects. It was from this illustration that Mother Shirley learned the importance of not criticizing others when they do things differently.

The "broad umbrella" principle gives structure to the value of unbiased love. It sets the parameters for her spiritual retreats allowing Protestants, Catholics, Charismatics and Orthodox all to worship together in harmony without one group judging another group. Mother Shirley attracts people of all denominations to her.

In Mother Shirley's life many times she experienced the anger and hatred directed toward her by another Christian. She cultivates unbiased love for these people by praying the following prayer, "Lord, create a need in their life that only I can meet. Then send me with love to meet that need." Years ago when Mother Shirley and Pop lived in a Mennonite community there was one elder who disliked her. There was a falling out with this particular elder holding a grudge against Shirley. She prayed that prayer and some years later he was forced to call Shirley out of desperation. He and his family were traveling and they had no money to stay in a hotel. He called and asked if his family could spend the night at Shirley's home. She recognized the situation as God putting him into her debt working out reconciliation.

Once she and a group of the sisters attended a conference at a church in which they knew one of the staff members. During the tour of the church, Mother Shirley made some observations about how the church valued and expressed some of their beliefs. The values of this particular church differed greatly from Shirley's values. Afterwards, she said, "I can worship with them, I must not criticize how they do things, but I don't have to walk with them."

In Sparta, Tennessee there is a small Christian book store. Mother Shirley frequented the store always buying many Bibles. The two ladies who worked there looked at Mother Shirley suspiciously since she wore a gray habit. They were cordial but distant. Mother Shirley was consistent in extending kindness toward them even though the kindness was not returned as they thought she was a Catholic. Approximately six months later one of the ladies asked Mother Shirley what she did with all of the Bibles she constantly bought. She explained how she was constantly sharing Jesus with people she met. For some reason that answer softened their hearts as she was no longer viewed as a threat.

Madame Guyon believed that it is God who brings people into our lives. She taught that it is the Christian's duty to love from the heart with unbiased love those people. God is answering Mother Shirley's prayer about being like her historical mentor, Madame Guyon.

Spiritual and Emotional Healing:

This focal value almost seems to be a by-product of the first two focal values. People often experience healing when they are in Mother Shirley's presence over an extended period of time. It is common to witness the healing that takes place in the lives of people who attend her spiritual retreats without receiving inner healing prayer. During worship people begin to weep. As the worship continues they experience a deep release of pain or shame or guilt. Others will gather around to minister and affirm what God is doing in their lives. The person receiving the ministry then experiences forgiveness and a sense of freedom from the prior troubles.

The value she abides by, that it is her job to love and the Holy Spirit's job to convict, contributes to the many people who experience healing through on-going interactions with her. She is a safe person to be around. Before I met Mother Shirley I believed that freedom from *entrenched* choices (whatever the choice may be) was not possible apart from receiving formal deliverance. After spending time with her and observing the power of manifest and unbiased love in the lives of those to whom she ministers, it seems that healing can be a natural outcome of the manifested love.

The Focal Value Braid:

Manifest love to the lost, Unbiased love to the church, and Healing

It seems that Mother Shirley is the essence of love as it is described in one set of her core chapters found in Matthew 5, 6, and 7. What makes her unique is that she is the living embodiment of the Sermon on the Mount. When the truths taught by Jesus in the Sermon on the Mount are actually lived out, it produces manifest and unbiased love which then births healing. Sometimes the healing occurs within the realm of the body, and/or the soul, and/or the spirit. What makes the manifest and unbiased love so powerful, coupled with the depth of healing it produces, is the persecution and suffering she endured for Christ primarily at the hands of other Christians over the course of many years. No cost was too great for her when it came to following Jesus. She never gave up. At times she was ready to quit the Church but never Jesus. Evangelism flows naturally from the love that exudes from her being so that she evangelizes as she goes about her business without ever being intentional. If you ever want to know what the love of Jesus looks like, watch Shirley.

FOCUSED LIFE OBSERVATIONS

Mother Shirley's Effective Methodologies Related to This Braid

- Frequent the same businesses in order to build relationships;
- Ask questions to open the door to conversations;
- Do not judge;
- Nurture babes in Christ as a mother nurtures a newborn = spend a lot of time with those new in the faith to grow them;
- Intentionally celebrate the majesty of God;
- She knows who she is called to – young adults and the military;
- One-on-one mentoring;
- Teaching small Bible studies as requested by the young adults;
- Meals together;
- Hospitality.

Quotes worth Remembering from Mother Shirley

1. Glean everywhere you go (even in a negative situation).
2. Don't be stuck and stupid!
3. My job is to love you; it is God's job to straighten you out!
4. Weed your own garden and stay out of others!
5. I'll see you in the plan! (This is a fare-well greeting which refers to the individual walking out God's plan in his/her life until they meet again.)
6. Repentance is the greatest gift God gave to me.
7. No man ever spoke as this man (referring to Jesus).
8. I'd rather sit on a street corner with a drunk or prostitute than in a church next to a religious hypocrite.
9. My pots and pans are just as holy as your (you fill in the blank)!
10. With every loss there is a gain.
11. When people don't give, don't follow them, you don't need to judge them, but don't follow them.
12. Rebuke negative thoughts not negative circumstances.
13. Faith is activated by choice.
14. Suffering is the only means to get to the glory.
15. God doesn't change, but after I walk with him for a while I will think differently about Him.
16. Everything man takes away from us, God supplies.
17. Others don't ruin your life, only you can ruin your life!
18. You cannot fight love.
19. Sometime in your life you have to decide what standard you will live by.
20. How can you love people who are nailing your feet to the cross? It sounds pretty, but it is hard.
21. He will touch exactly what you hold on to the greatest!
22. He always gives something back that is greater.
23. Never leave a place until God tells you to leave.
24. You can't minister when it is convenient for you, you must minister when the need arises.
25. Faith is activated by choice.
26. In Christ there are no leftovers – everyday you get new!
27. Not having anything is not victory. Not wanting anything is victory.

Ministry Insights into Sphere of Influence & Spiritual Authority

Shirley's spiritual authority and sphere of influence developed simultaneously. It should be noted that her spiritual authority and sphere of influence continue to increase as she transitions into convergence.[54] The negative processing incidences, her radical obedience, and the manifest and unbiased love she nurtured her whole life all contributed

[54] This terms refers to that advanced stage of a leader's life when giftedness, spiritual authority, sphere of influence, maturity, location, sense of destiny all converge which produces maximum ministry effectiveness.

to increasing her spiritual authority. She never sought spiritual authority. Rather it is a by-product of her focus on Christ. Clinton defines spiritual authority as,

> That characteristic of a God-anointed leader developed upon an experiential power base which enables a leader to influence followers through persuasion, force of modeling and moral expertise toward God's purposes. (Clinton 1989:192)[55]

Shirley's non-defensive posture and integrity enabled her to maturely deal the negative processing incidences in her life. That approach provided Mother Shirley a solid experiential power base from which to lead. The negative processing she encountered in her life involved the use of coercive and manipulative authority exerted by others upon her. In the midst of her negative processing incidences she engaged personal authority to govern her behavior. Personal authority is rooted in the possessor's character. Often personal authority appears non-existent when confronted by manipulation or coercive authority. Her right responses to negative experiences increased her spiritual authority.

According to Clinton there are three kinds of influence: 1. Direct which is face to face and is bounded by time; 2. Indirect which happens through other mediums such as printed or electronic means and is not bounded by time; and 3. Organizational in which an individual exerts influence upon all within the organization.[56]

At present, she exerts two types of influence: direct, and organizational. For the most part, her sphere of influence mirrors her ultimate contributions[57] which are discussed in the next section. She is a mentor in which influence is primarily direct. As a founder, she uses organizational influence upon those following her. Her lack of indirect influence shapes and limits her ultimate contribution of promoter. Family is primarily limited to the direct sphere of influence.

This biography will help to expand Shirley's sphere of influence to include the indirect domain. When God wants to expand the influence base of a non-writer, he sends others to come along side of that leader to do just that. Also, if the Order of the Myrrhbearers continues after Shirley's death, that will transition her from direct to indirect influence organizationally.

God continues to increase her direct sphere of influence. For example, a few months ago a female General observed her influence upon a group of people she did not know during the Friday welcome of the wounded vets at the Pentagon. This General wanted to meet Mother Shirley. When the General discovered that she was praying for another General, she asked if Mother Shirley would pray for her on an ongoing consistent basis. One can see how God trained her to be in a position of influence with Generals.

She learned how to steward authority properly with personal authority which is based in one's character. At this point in her life, convergence is beginning to happen. Her capacity as a leader is large, that is why people feel the essence of love and authority

---

[55] For a more in-depth examination on spiritual authority refer to Dr. Clinton's book, **Leadership Emergence Theory,** pages 192-197. As stated earlier, Shirley never pursued spiritual authority. She was always submissive to those in authority over her. Whenever she was expelled, she was not defensive but quietly left.

[56] Dr. Clinton goes into greater detail about organizational influence in his book, **Leadership Emergence Theory**, on page 228.

[57] According to Dr. Clinton an ultimate contribution is the legacy that a leader leaves behind. Dr. Clinton categorizes thirteen different kinds of ultimate contributions. For more information refer to chapter six in Dr. Clinton's book, **Strategic Concepts.**

when they are in her presence. God is dove-tailing her capacity as a leader with the people he wants her to influence. Since she has developed great spiritual authority she is able to influence in a godly way.

Contributions

This study contributes to the general field of leadership development in the following ways:

1. Her life illustrates that leaders are not to seek spiritual authority. She never sought it instead she sought the Lord embracing the posture that no cost is too great. Leaders should seek the Lord. It is up to God to grant spiritual authority.

2. As a leader, gender was not an issue in her obedience to God. Other people had an issue with her gender and the spiritual gifts that God gave to her, but she did not use her gender to determine how and when she should obey.

3. Her life reveals that sometimes God will prepare a future leader even before that leader knows him.

4. God will use one's circumstances, positive and negative, to shape that leader for his/her calling. Mother Shirley grew up as an emotional orphan. Today, she is called to mother other emotional orphans.

5. God grew her sphere of influence over the years. Rejected by man, declared a Jezebel by pastors, and kicked out of churches did not diminish her sphere of influence. Today she has greater influence than when she experienced those injustices at the hands of others, because her response honored the Lord.

6. Success comes when a leader stays within his/her calling. Focus, Focus, Focus!

Ultimate Contribution Set

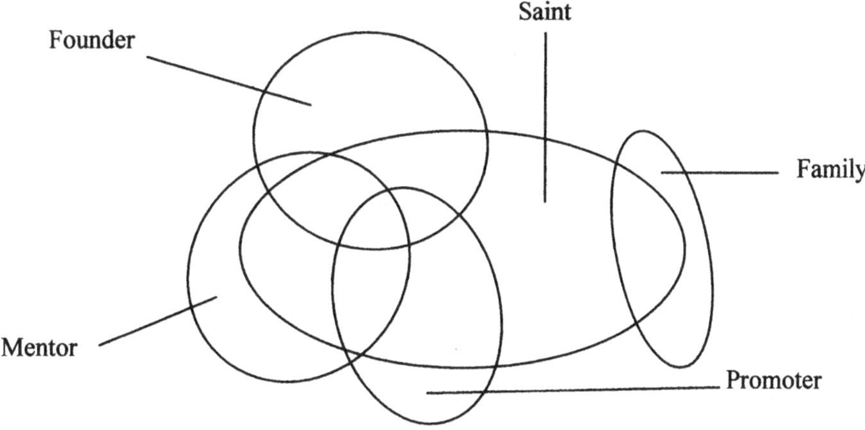

A summary of her ultimate contribution reveals that she has two ultimate contributions in the character category which reveals a strong character development in her life over the years. She has one ultimate contribution in the ministry, organizational, and ideation categories. The only category missing is the catalytic. It is fifty years too early to see if she will qualify in regard to the religious Order of the Myrrhbearers she established. Ignatius of Loyola who established the Jesuits never set out to establish a religious world order. He saw a need and fulfilled it.

The categories listed below are listed in the order in which Dr. Clinton listed them on the Ultimate Contribution chart and not in order of prominence in her life.

First and foremost she is a **Saint.** Shirley never set out to become a saint. She grew incrementally as she sought God in how to live her life. The title of this biography, ***No Cost to Great*** reflects the intensity of her search in order to live a life congruent with the teaching of the scriptures. The overarching thrust of her focal values, unbiased love for the Church and manifest love to the lost combined with her willingness to pay any cost in order to follow the Lord propels her into the category of saint. She models 1 Corinthians 13. As a result, generals and murderers and people in between want to emulate the qualities lived out in her life.

Shirley had no positive role models to show her how to raise a **Family** that honors God. The lack of modeling intensified her desire to raise a family that loved and honored God. The intense persecution that she experienced negatively affected some of her children making them wander away from God for a season. She never preached at them, but she did pray. It was her unbiased love toward her children when some of them made poor decisions that eventually drew them back into relationship with the Lord. Today all of her children follow the Lord.

Mother Shirley's skills in mothering make her a **Mentor** extraordinaire! Her primary methods of mentoring are through teaching one on one, in small study group settings, larger group settings such as her retreats, or in modeling love as she interacts with those who cross her path. There is a constant stream of people traveling from out of state just to spend a few days with her. Many times her guests are not able to articulate the reason driving them to see her. The effectiveness of her mentoring rests in her ability to practice both manifest and unbiased love. Because of that quality in her life, people grant her permission to speak truth into their lives even if the truth is unpleasant and hard.

Because people grant Mother Shirley permission to speak into their lives, they are willing to follow her in new endeavors. Mother Shirley's passion and ability to see needs and articulate those needs in proper venues qualify her as a **Founder.** The sisterhood she founded and the spiritual retreats she hosts came about through recognizing and fulfilling a need. She stumbled upon a problem, and had the foresight and leadership skills to meet the previously unidentified need at the time. The first ministry Shirley established resulted from watching the football game and recognizing the need of the Church to celebrate the majesty and splendor of God. She saw a need and set about organizing the teams of people needed to fulfill that need within the Church. These dance teams were invited to perform in many different venues.

The second ministry was the founding of the Orthodox Order of the Myrrhbearers (originally named The Franciscan Order of the Cloistered Heart) also was incidental. Mother Shirley, Jackie, and a few other friends wanted to create a community which would be a safe haven for their children to grow up in the Lord. The original focus was for their children. Now that their children are gown and the order is growing in numbers, the focus has shifted somewhat. To be a member one must be willing to be in community with the Sisters and Brothers, and to pursue God. These two foci are expressed through the annual spiritual retreat.

Every founder needs a promoter. When Shirley sees a need to establish a new work (founder) she becomes a powerful promoter. Shirley has a presence about her. She exudes both love and a strong leadership style. Some even equate her skills and giftedness to that of an Army Command Sergeant Major. That combination may seem contradictory but in reality it is not. People respond to her because of her love and are inspired action because of the aura of leadership that exudes from her. Both extremes balance each other out. That combination makes her a powerful **Promoter.** When she had the new idea about the need to celebrate the splendor of God, people were ready to join her in this expressive way of celebrating the presence of God.

Giftedness Development

Implications for a Focused Life

Venn diagram – Focal Element: Spiritual Gifts

Key: *Italicized* spiritual gifts, natural abilities and acquired skills are not included in the Venn diagram. They are listed for reference only.

Spiritual Gifts: Only the top gifts are included in the Venn Diagram.			**Natural Abilities**	**Acquired Skills**
Word Gifts	**Love Gifts**	**Power Gifts**		
Teaching Exhortation Ruling *Prophecy* *Pastor*	Mercy *Giving*	*Word of Wisdom* *Discerning of Spirits* *Tongues*	Organizational skills Relational Skills	Cooking Iconography *Artistic Abilities*
○	○	○	□	△

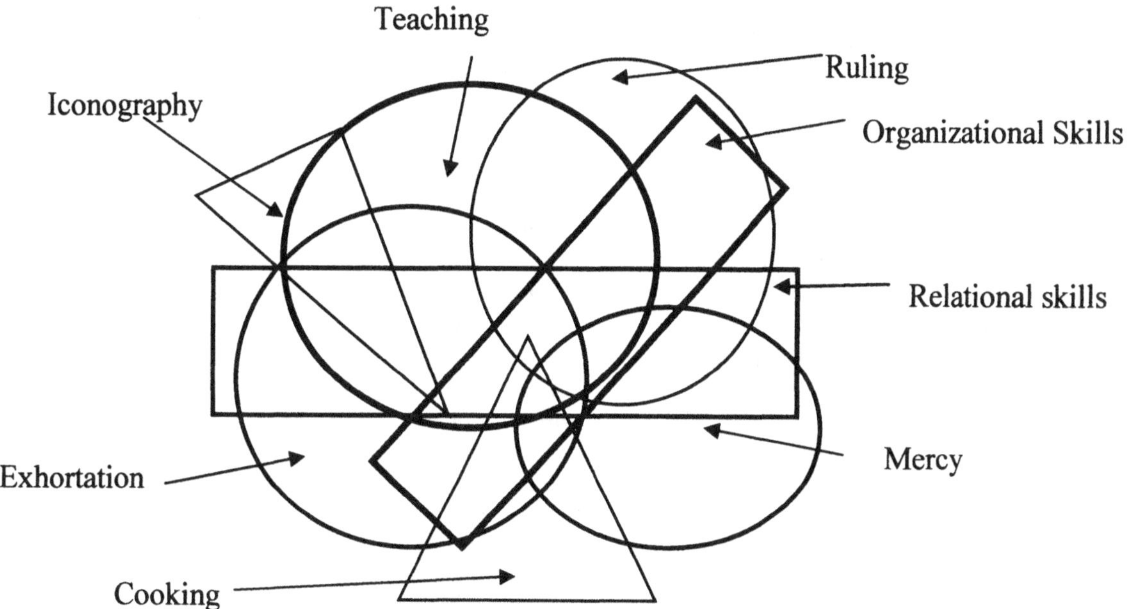

A tight Venn diagram reflects stronger giftings, natural talents, and acquired skills. It is clear that Mother Shirley ministers out of her giftedness. Her focal element is spiritual gifts with teaching, exhortation, and mercy as dominate spiritual gifts. Her three core values that drive her ministry focus are healing, unbiased love for the Church and unbiased love for the lost. These values are expressed through her strong gift of mercy. Teaching is the strongest gift because she teaches in whatever venue she finds herself. What makes her teaching powerful is how she combines it with her gift of mercy. People feel loved; and therefore, they are open to listening and learning from her at a level of acceptance.

Her acquired skills and natural talents supplement her gift of mercy in ministry settings. Her relational skills include her ability to use humor effectively and, at the same time, to "tell it like it is" without being judgmental or critical of the person.

Destiny Processing and Type

The purpose of destiny processing[58] is to recognize the shaping hand of God upon the person throughout that his or her life. Through reflection destiny processing allows the person to see the process God used to develop and position the person to enter into destiny fulfillment. In Shirley's case, God began preparing her before she knew the calling on her life. The Ministry Foundation Stage[59] set the emotions and the longings for her future calling. In the General Ministry Stage[60] she received destiny affirmation concerning her call. In the Convergence Stage she is experiencing the fulfillment of the affirmation from the previous stage.

Another purpose of compiling a destiny chart is that of encouragement. It allows the recipient and others know that God is in control even when it may appear that he is not in control at times. Moreover, it increases faith in God and gratitude toward him for how he works all things together for the good of those who believe and follow him (Romans 8:28).

Time-line Position	Destiny Label	Processing Incident	Type
PHASE I Sub-phase A Ministry Foundations	Emotional Orphan	Destiny Preparation: ***Hints at future calling to the marginalized***	Type II: Indirect
PHASE I Sub-phase A Ministry Foundations	Candy Bar	Destiny Preparation: ***Established value of generosity***	Type II: Indirect
PHASE I Sub-phase A Ministry Foundations	God, are you up there?	Destiny Preparation: ***Hints at future role in intercession***	Type IA: Unusual Encounter with God
PHASE I Sub-phase A Ministry Foundations	Patriotic & military Song	Destiny Preparation: ***Hints at future role in praying for the military***	Type III: Providential
PHASE II Sub-phase A General Ministry	His Eye is on the Sparrow	Destiny Revelation: ***Defined intensity of calling upon life***	Type IB: Awe Inspiring Revelation
PHASE II Sub-phase A General Ministry	Please teach the elders!	Destiny Revelation: ***Hints at future role in teaching leaders/men***	Type III: Providential

---

[58] Dr. Clinton defines four types of destiny experiences. The first one is awe-inspiring which can be either an unusual encounter with God or an awe-inspiriting revelation from God. The second one is indirect meaning that the person receiving the destiny experience does so through another person. The third type is called providential because it is an accumulation of past experiences where the leader realizes that he/she should be doing something based upon the accumulation. The last one is referred to as a blessing. The leader senses the powerful presence of God in his or her life and ministry. The evidence of God's blessing suggests a strong sense of destiny upon the person.

[59] The Ministry Foundation Stage is the first stage on the ministry time-line. During this stage character and personality develops. Often the future leader experiences first steps in ministry. For more information on Ministry Foundation Stage see Dr. Clinton's book, **Strategic Concepts**, page 9.

[60] The General Ministry is the second PHASE on the ministry time-line. In this PHASE the leader experiments with ministry and discovering his/her giftedness in the process. Competency is gain in the later stages of this second PHASE. For more information on the General Ministry Stage see Dr. Clinton's book, **Strategic Concepts**, page 9.

PHASE II Sub-phase A and B General Ministry	Substitute Preacher	Destiny Revelation: ***Hints at future role of pastor***	Type III: Providential
PHASE II Sub-phase C General Ministry	Mother of Israel	Destiny Revelation: ***Defines kind of calling***	Type II: Indirect
PHASE II Sub-phase B General Ministry	Football Game	Destiny Revelation: ***Defines Effective Methodology***	Type IB: Awe Inspiring Revelation
PHASE II Sub-phase General Ministry	POW Bracelet	Destiny Revelation: ***Reveals ministry to military & prisoners***	Type IB: Awe Inspiring Revelation
PHASE IV Sub-phase A Focused Ministry	Radio Show	Destiny Fulfillment: ***Beginning fulfillment of ministry to military***	Type III: Providential
PHASE IV Sub-phase A Focused Ministry	Genesis 35:1-11	Destiny Fulfillment: ***The habit attracts people because she is perceived as motherly***	Type IB: Awe Inspiring Revelation
PHASE V Sub-phase B Convergent Ministry	Syrian Orthodox Priesthood	Destiny Fulfillment: ***Pastor role officially to be confirmed***	Type IV: Blessing of God

Identification of Key Ministry Insights

This was covered in Mother Shirley's Focal Value Braid approach to ministry: manifest love to the lost, unbiased love to the Church, and healing to all.

Identification of Major Values That Uniquely Fit Her Ministry

Number	Value	Context
1.	A leader must not make decisions for other people.	An inmate asked Mother Shirley if a person can be a homosexual and a Christian.
2.	A believer should follow those who are generous.	As an early Christian she asked God how she could tell the difference between false and true prophets. This value was her answer.
3.	A leader ought not to dishonor the name of the Lord.	Christians who do not leave generous tips at the restaurant dishonor the name of the Lord. They portray a stingy God when in reality God is generous.
4.	A leader must be bold irregardless of the cost.	Mother Shirley learned the cost of worshipping the Lord in a church that valued conformity and rigidness before the Lord.
5.	A leader should focus on Jesus and not the problem.	This value reflects the same value of Madame Guyon, her historical mentor.
6.	A leader ought to praise God when feeling down.	God does not give his children thoughts to discourage them
7.	A leader should glean	Mother Basilea's taught that one ought not to be

	everywhere he or she goes!	critical of others.
8.	A Christian should be available when others need them.	Availability value – when problems happen Christians should be ready to help others in the time of their need.
9.	Scripture must take precedence over culture, even Christian culture.	Mother Shirley learned this value early in her Christian walk when she learned about demons at a time when most of the Church believed that demons were not present in the United States.
10.	A believer ought to believe God over and above all others.	Insight gained early in her Christian walk when the husbands of the women who attended Mother Shirley's bible study at the mall told their wives that she had no spiritual covering. Mother Shirley prayed and God told her he was her spiritual covering.

Integration of Personality Factors That Identifies a Focused or Ideal Role Which Moves the Leader toward Convergence

Years ago Shirley received a prophetic word that she was a mother in Israel. The development of her personality through the years supports that prophetic word. If people had to describe her using three primary words they would say motherly, loving, and strong-willed. She sets the pace for whatever endeavor in which she finds herself. She exudes love in such a way that it is possible to sense an aura of love about her. Last, she is strong-willed which complements her leadership abilities. The term "mother" symbolizes one who has authority and one who teaches. The symbolic use of the term "mother," refers to mothers who are balanced and honorable.

People who are marginalized need a loving mother to speak into their lives. Mothers and grandmothers are often known for their non-ceasing intercession for their children. Her personality carries with it all of the qualities needed to command respect by those in the military. The examination of Mother Shirley's life clearly shows that God prepared her, called her, and then transformed her personality to fit the role he pre-ordained for her.

Social Base Processing

The release pattern would best describe Shirley and Bill's social base[61]. Bill worked outside of the home freeing Shirley to do ministry at times as a lay person and at other times in a professional capacity. Shirley functions as a strong leader in every endeavor in which she finds herself. When it comes to ministry, she leads and Bill willingly participates and supports her financially, emotionally, and spiritually through his prayers for her and his blessing of her leadership.

---

[61] The social base refers to four components that comprise one's home-base. Through examining one's social, emotional, physical (adequate food, clothing, etc.), strategic, and economic base can one's social base be determined. For further study see Dr. Clinton's **Leadership Emergence Theory** book, chapter four.

Ultimate Contribution Set

In summary, Mother Shirley's five main areas of contribution are as a saint, mentor, founder, promoter, and family.

Ministry Philosophy Concepts

Mother Shirley never formalized her ministry philosophy. However, she does have a ministry philosophy and it is expressed primarily through her many quotes from which her principles and values are derived. Her ministry philosophy would mirror that of Madame Guyon and Mother Basilea. All three have lived out the philosophy that no cost is too great in following the Lord.

Future Perfect Time Paradigm

Mother Shirley did not operate out of a future perfect time paradigm.[62] She was not aware of destiny unfolding in her life as she lived it. Her focus was always on the present and living a holy life by applying God's truths to her life circumstances as events unfolded. By writing this biography it is easy to see the destiny threads unfold in her life.

[62] Dr. Clinton defines future perfect paradigm as "a way of seeing something in the future as thought it were real. Such a view dominates what one does and perceives. All activity moves towards the actual realization of the already felt reality" (Clinton 1995b:53).

Boundary Processing[63]

PHASE	Boundary Name	Type	Reason
PHASE I	Emotional orphan	**Surprise:** This kind of boundary is sudden requiring an immediate decision. Shirley's doctor encouraged her to divorce her first husband right after the birth of her second child. She followed through within a few months.	After the birth of her second son, her doctor encouraged Shirley to divorce her first husband. As a doctor he was concerned about her mental health because her current husband was not a good man. Divorce was considered a stigma in the 1950's, but she still did it. After the divorce, she re-met Bill a year later and was married in two years.
PHASE II	Formal Rejection	**Surprise:** The decision by the elders to kick Shirley out of the church totally surprised both Bill and Shirley.	She had just received the spiritual gift of tongues. The church in which she and Bill attended taught cessationism. The church also believed that women could not teach men, only women and children. The baptist church made an exception for a while because more men and women attended the church to be in her Sunday school class. However, the church was a glass ceiling and God orchestrated this move by the elders to kick her out so that she would be free to attend a church in which she could develop her spiritual gifts.
PHASE III	Loss = Gain	**Growth:** This kind of boundary happens when the individual (this time Bill) needs a change in order to grow. When they lost the $256,000, Shirley said that was a wonderful day because he had an encounter with God.	Over the period of two years Bill lost $256,000 due to some bad decisions. They also lost their nice home. Shirley felt that God allowed this loss to get Bill's attention and He did! As a result of this loss, they had to move. This move transitioned Shirley into a new role of mother.
PHASE IV	The Promise Land at last!	**Expansion:** This type of boundary means that the person was not being challenged in the previous PHASE and God allows the boundary to increase sphere of influence due to new levels of ministry.	Bill travels during the week with his job, but he comes home on the weekends. In 2002, Mother Shirley got sick during the week while Bill was traveling for his job. This made her daughter Holly, realize her parents needed to be closer to family. Due to this move Shirley is transitioning into convergence and the beginning stages of afterglow.

[63] Boundaries are associated with the time-line. The time-line is divided according to PHASES or major themes defined by time. For most people the first PHASE is comprised of childhood until the child leaves home. The second PHASE usually is comprised of early ministry activities. As a person progresses toward convergence (late in life) one can see the PHASES becoming more focused. Within each PHASE there are sub-phases which comprise the PHASE. According to Clinton a boundary is the label given to the time immediately preceding the end of a sub-phase of PHASE which usually is made up of an entry stage, transition stage, and termination stage. God uses the boundary to free the person from one PHASE so that the person is free to enter into a new PHASE. The boundary happens within the last sub-phase of the PHASE and initiates the beginning of the new PHASE.

By placing these boundaries in a chart, it is easy to see how God orchestrated circumstances to reposition Shirley for the next PHASE of her growth as a leader and as a person.

Paradigm Shifts Narrowing the Focus

Shirley experienced many paradigm shifts. Three strategic ones are included here. These three paradigm shifts set the focus of her pursuit of God and how she viewed ministry.

1. **"It's not about what we get; it's about what we give."**
This paradigm formed early in her ministry during PHASE II. It grew out of a concern Shirley had of following a false prophet. When she was a new Christian, she realized she did not know the scriptures well enough nor did she have the maturity to recognize good leaders from bad leaders. She prayed and asked God to show her how to distinguish the good Christian leaders (Christ-focused) from the bad Christian leaders (self-focused). She felt God impressed upon her that any leader who was genuinely generous, without selfish motives, was safe to follow. From that prayer interaction with God she formed the paradigm that good leaders are generous. This paradigm complements her calling to be a mother to all. People deprived of love and nurture over an extended period of time become emotional orphans. They need love, affirmation, and someone to delight in their presence. Because of this paradigm of generosity, Mother Shirley leaves large tips for the waiters and waitresses. That opens the doors to friendship. She lavishes love and complements to all she sees throughout the day, and on all she knows. The military is structured to give and to put their lives on the lines for others. They need to be supported by others who will give to them. The paradigm of generosity that guides Mother Shirley's actions directs her in giving liberally to those in the military she knows through prayer, love, and encouragement. Mother Shirley does not limit generosity to the giving to gifts. She is generous with the tangibles and the intangibles such as love and encouragement.
2. **The Church without walls**
This paradigm formed at the beginning of PHASE III. After Shirley was kicked out of the baptist church, she realized that the Church is not the actual building located on a physical piece of property, but it is comprised of believers. This transformed her thinking. It also complemented her life calling because many emotional orphans do not attend the traditional church located on a physical piece of property. They are outside of the church and have no desire to attend. Her paradigm shift freed her to minister to them where they are.[64]
3. **"My job is to love you; it is God's job to straighten you out!**
This paradigm formed at the end of PHASE IV. It crystallized while she ministered to the female inmates at the Tennessee Women's Prison. The shift increased her spiritual authority, her influence, and her ability to heal the emotional hurts of others through manifest and unbiased love of God. This paradigm allowed her to understand

[64] This illustrates what Dr. Clinton describes as the "Starting-Point-Plus processing. The paradigm shift to view the Church without walls embraces this model of meeting people where they are. For more information on this process refer to an article Dr. Clinton wrote and published, *Gender and Leadership: My Personal Journey.*

her role in the process and the role of the Holy Spirit in the ministry process. Before this paradigm she was judgmental of people.

Summary on Focused Life Insights from Her Life

Dr. Clinton describes a focused life as "a life dedicated exclusively to carrying out God's unique purposes through it.[65]" This definition describes Shirley's life journey. Dr. Clinton goes on to state that a focused life is accomplished through the following:

- By identifying the focal issues, that is, the major role, life purpose, unique methodology, or ultimate contribution.
- An increasing prioritization of life's activities around the focal issues.

This description of a focused life applies to Mother Shirley. She lives a focused life.

[65] For a more in-depth study on this topic of living a focused life refer to Clinton's book, **Strategic Concepts that Clarify a Focused Life**, page 2.

OVERVIEW OF A FOCUSED LIFE

Life Purpose

In her own words, "Restoring God's manifest love to the body of Christ."

Major Role

Her major roles are mother to all, teacher, mentor, leader, and intercessor.

Effective Methodology

The following list contains some of Mother Shirley's effective methodologies that defined her as a leader.
Effective Methodologies are those ministry insights that enable one to carry out his or her life purpose and become an effective medium by which to accomplish it.

1. 1968 The Power of Mentoring
Mother Shirley began mentoring early in her Christian walk. She mentors one-on-one or in small groups such as Bible Studies. Her mentoring is informal in nature. Much of her mentoring is done through hospitality where people will come and stay with her for several days and leave refreshed. People usually find perspective as they listen to her speak. She fulfills the mentor role of spiritual guide, counselor, teacher, divine contact, and contemporary model. Teaching the icon classes fulfills the role of coach and teacher.
Effective Methodology: Even though she ***mentors informally*** she uses mentoring effectively.

2. 1969 Spiritual Retreats
The purpose of Mother Shirley's spiritual retreats is to celebrate the majesty and splendor of God. The retreats are also an avenue for people to renew their covenantal relationship with God. Currently Mother Shirley hosts these annual spiritual retreats with her Myrrhbearers Order. In 1969 she watched a half-time show during a football game with her children. She decided then that the Church needed to celebrate the Lord in a similar fashion. Her spiritual retreats are different from retreats other churches host. The focus is to celebrate the majesty of God with intentionality. She does this through choreograph dance, artistically decorated surroundings that support the theme for the year, and by giving away many small spiritual gifts and spiritual words.
Effective Methodology: Provide a venue for people to experience the splendor of God so that they can ***renew their covenantal relationship*** with Christ through a ***retreat experience***.

3. 1970 Parable Teller
Mother Shirley knows how to communicate truth powerfully through the use of stories. Telling parables was an effective methodology Jesus used. Shirley also communicates truth through the use of parables: however, the parables that she tells are her own true-life stories. She is a master story-teller, able to hold captive her audience as she illustrates important Biblical truths through the disasters, failures, and triumphs of her life

Effective Methodology: Provide a bridge that allows people to see what the truth in God's word looks like as it is lived out in one's life. Shirley's parable telling does that.

4. 1970 Teaching Bible Studies

Mother Shirley is a teacher-leader. After her salvation she began teaching. She was effective in her teaching as her classes were always full. Her presentation of truth is clear and powerful, so that people not only understand it, but also able to apply it to their lives. ***Effective Methodology:*** She uses an informal ***class format*** as her venue to teach. She taught Sunday school classes, and Bible studies in non-religious-structures like the state prison. She currently teaches Bible studies in her home.

5. 1973 Processionals

The processionals were comprised of dance teams, flag teams, tambourine teams and sword teams (for men). The teams had beautiful costumes and would choreograph their routines. Mother Shirley's teams were invited to participate in parades, conferences, military bases, and retreats. In response to the processionals many people would make comments like, "I didn't want to come to this today. I was so sick of the Christmas stuff. I don't approve of so much of it, but you have renewed my faith in Christmas today." The renewal thrust[66] of the processionals set them apart from others.
Effective Methodology: Mother Shirley effectively used celebratory pageantry through ***dance teams, flag teams, tambourine teams, and sword teams*** performing all over the United States. These performances enabled people to grasp the splendor of the holiness of the Lord.

6. 1974 Home Bible Studies

Mother Shirley commented through her interview that she and Bill always had a Bible study in their home. This is one of her effective methodologies. The current Bible study in her home begins with a group dinner, the dinner creates community. The young people usually stay until 11 p.m. or mid-night just asking questions and listening as Mother Shirley teaches. Some of her home-Bible studies are at night and others have been during the daytime.
Effective Methodology*:** Mother Shirley uses a ***pedagogical[67] approach to her bible studies. Her ***teaching is exhortative in nature***. She effectively uses personal stories illustrating and confirming the validity of God's word.

7. 1977 Community Life Groups

This happened by accident. A woman who attended one of her bible studies at the mall, wanted to move her family closer to Mother Shirley. The woman wanted to spend more time with her. As a result, the woman sold her home, but she could not find another home to buy. Mother Shirley invited her family to move into their recently purchased

---

[66] Mother Shirley wanted to create an atmosphere at the retreat, where one could reconnect with God in an experiential way. When she first started hosting these retreats, they were different because at that time, most retreats focused on imparting knowledge. Imparting knowledge was not the primary purpose of her retreats. Teaching was held to a minimum. Worship was emphasized through pageantry. Many participants often expressed feeling refreshed after attending one of Mother Shirley's retreats.

[67] Pedagogy refers to teacher oriented learning. The students respond by learning what the teacher teaches. The teacher imparts knowledge. The student learns the knowledge.

home until they could find a home to buy. Within a couple of months there were nineteen people living in a small one bathroom home. This community life group gave Mother Shirley a paradigm shift as she no longer viewed the Church from the perspective of a church building. She now viewed the Church as beyond the building. The community life group lasted one year of everyone living in community. This is listed as an effective methodology because this perspective of community under girded the formation of the sisterhood. Additionally, it informs the dynamic creating the house church located in the small chapel next to Mother Shirley's home.
Effective Methodology: Community is covenantal in nature. ***Community life groups*** are an effective methodology of Mother Shirley's because wherever she goes it seems that she starts a new community life group.

8. 1987 Orthodox Order of the Myrrhbearers of the Cloistered Heart
This group also started incidentally. A group of mothers were meeting together in a bible study and decided that they needed to form an actual community as a spiritual point of reference for their children. The Cloistered Heart Sisterhood began as a Catholic order but recently became an Orthodox order. They have officers and sacred rules of life governing them. This group is growing. At this time, there is only the one chapter.
Effective Methodology: This ***sister and brotherhood order*** establishes accountability and community for those who desire to pursue Christ within the sister and brotherhood.

9. 2002 As You Go Evangelism
This is an incidental ministry. It seems that wherever Mother Shirley regularly frequents people come to know the Lord through her love and genuine interest in their lives. Many of the people who attend her church are the servers and the owners from the restaurants she frequents. She is not intentional in her evangelism as some are, she just loves people wherever she goes.
Effective Methodology: Frequent the same business locales so that relationships can be established. What makes her genuine is that she loves people whether or not they accept Christ.

Ultimate Contribution: Drift

The drift label refers to a "step by step guidance fashion. There is no purposeful deliberate attempt to have an ultimate contribution. The person simply follows what he/she thinks is God's guidance. Dr. Clinton writes, "Each major guidance decision will probably lead to some new accomplishment that will be the focus of efforts until God gives guidance for the next phase."[68] This describes Shirley's journey toward her ultimate contribution. She never experienced a profound revelation of her life calling as a child. Instead, she just obediently followed the Lord step by step, keeping her eyes on the ground, as directed by Psalms 119:105, "Your word is a lamp to my feet and a light for my path (NIV)."

[68] (Clinton 1995b:163)

CONCLUSION

Now that Hebrews 13:7-8 is fulfilled by remembering Mother Shirley, it is important to complete this memory by learning from her life. Her life models how to:

- Love the lost with manifest love;
- Love the Church with unbiased love;
- Pay the cost in knowing Jesus;
- Allow God to be our defender;
- Never tell God that it is too hard to depend upon Him;
- Let the Holy Spirit convict;
- Obey God even when it is culturally wrong;
- Understand that the essence of leadership is not gender-based;
- Persevere and never give up!

For Further Study

1. Study the life and teachings of Madame Guyon as Mother Shirley's life mirrors her life.

2. Study the life and teachings of Mother Basilea. For more information write to: Canaan In The Desert, 9849 N. 40th St., Phoenix, AZ 85028-4099

3. Study how Saint Patrick of Ireland practiced evangelism as Mother Shirley's method is similar.

4. This is the first biography written about Mother Shirley. For that reason, there are no other resources available on her life or teachings. Hopefully that will change over time. If you would like more information about the Order of the Myrrhbearers, you can write to:

   Order of the Myrrhbearers
   Mother Shirley
   186 Mimi's Lane
   Sparta, Tennessee
   38582

   You can email Mother Shirley at habbaruth@yahoo.com

5. Read Clinton's article on *"Gender and Leadership: My Personal Pilgrimage"* in order to gain a better grasp on how God views leadership in light of gender available from Barnabas Publishers.

APPENDIX A: Timeline for Mother Shirley

"No Cost Too Great"

PHASE I: Emotional Orphan	PHASE II: Adopted by God	PHASE III: Nurtured by God	PHASE IV: Mother to All	PHASE V Afterglow
1933	1958	1974	1983	2002
Age:	25	41	50	69

PHASE I	PHASE II	PHASE III	PHASE IV	PHASE V
1933-1958 **Emotional Orphan** **1933-1958**	**Adopted by God** **1958-1974**	**Nurtured by God** **1974-1983**	**Mother to All** **1983 -2002**	**Afterglow** **2002 – to present**
1. Sub-phase A: **1933-1948** **Longing to Belong**	**1. Sub-phase A** **1958-1966** **Accepted by God**	**1. Sub-phase A:** **1974-1977** **Church without Walls**	**1. Sub-phase A:** **1983-1987** **Mother to the Abused**	**1. Sub-phase A:** **2000- 2006** **Healing Touch**
2. Sub-phase B: **1948-1954** **Accepted then Rejected**	**2. Sub-phase B** **1966-1971** **Formed by God**	**2. Sub-phase B:** **1977-1983** **Holy Mathematics**	**2. Sub-phase B:** **1987-1991** **Franciscan Order of the Cloistered Heart**	**2. Sub-phase B:** **2006 -** **Order of the Myrrhbearers Grows**
3. Sub-phase C: **1954-1958** **Accepted by Man...**	**3. Sub-phase C** **1971-1974** **Rejected by Man**		**3. Sub-phase C:** **1991-1998** **Mother to All Denominations**	
			4. Sub-phase D **1998-2002** **Mother to the Rejected**	

Critical Incidents in PHASE I:	Critical Incidents in PHASE II:	Critical Incidents in PHASE III:	Critical Incidents in PHASE IV:	Critical Incidents in PHASE V:
C-1: The Candy Bar	**C-4: Salvation**	**C-8: Honor Others**	**C-13: Abandoned**	**C-15: Mar-Michael**
C-2: Military Hymns	**C-5: Keswick Conferences**	**C-9: My Sin Hurts Others**	**C-14: 1-Bathroom Community!**	
C-3: God, are you out there?	**C-6: Celebrate!**	**C-10: Mother Basilea**		
	C-7: POW Bracelet	**C-11: Purged**		
		C-12: Heart Attack		

APPENDIX B: Glossary

Afterglow:	Fallout effects of a life well lived: spiritual authority dominate. (Clinton 1995b:9)
Base Plus Advance:	A leader should build upon past studies and advance them at each new opportunity. (Clinton 1997:167)
Boundary:	Is the label given to the time immediately preceding the end of a sub-phase or phase which usually is made up of an entry stage, transition stage, and termination stage. (Clinton 1989:305)
Cessationism:	The belief that the charismatic spiritual gifts ceased when the last original disciple of Jesus died. (Grudem 1996:42-43)
Core Set:	A core set is a collection of very important Bible books, usually from 5-20, which are or have been extremely meaningful to you in your life and for which you feel a burden from God to use with great power over and over in your ministry in the years to come. (Clinton 1997:xii)
Core Selection:	Refers to important passages, key biographical characters, special psalms, special parables, special values or key topics which are or have been extremely meaningful to you in your own life and for which you feel a burden from God to use with great power over and over in your ministry in the years to come. (Clinton 1997:xii)
Contemporary Mentor:	Is the technical term for a living person whose life or ministry, at least in part, is used as an example to indirectly impart skills, lessons of life and ministry, and values which empower another person. (Clinton & Clinton 1991:9-7)
Convergence:	An advanced PHASE along the generic time-line of a leader in which the leader experiences an increased effectiveness in ministry due to the coming together of a number of factors including giftedness, role, maturity, cogent ministry philosophy, sense of destiny, ideal influence-mix, geographical locale, special opportunity. (Clinton 1995a:486)
Crisis Process Item P (CR)[69]:	Refers to those special intense situations of pressure in human situations which are used by God to test and teach dependence. (Clinton 1989:210)
Destiny Preparation Process Item P (DP):	Describes a grouping of process items concerning a significant acts, people, providential circumstances, or timing, which hint at some future or special significance to a life and, when studied in retrospect, add firmness to a growing awareness of sense or destiny in a leader's life. (Clinton 1995a:103)
Direct Influence:	It is bounded by time meaning that the influence is exerted upon the other individual while being in the presence of the one exerting the influence. (Clinton 1989:228)

[69] Dr. Clinton created equations to identify what he labels "process items." Process items refer to the situations in a person's life God uses to development leadership skills. For more information see Dr. Clinton's book, **Leadership Emergence Theory**, chapter 4.

Divine Contact: A special kind of mentor who appears at a timely moment and intervenes in the life of a leader to impart information, perspective, direction, resources or whatever so as to significantly affect the leader usually in a strategic sense and does so with what is perceived as God-given authority. (Clinton 1995a:487)

Dynamic Reflection: A two-fold thinking process which teaches how to correlate input ideas relevantly to experience and formation on the one hand, and on the other, the thinking processes which draw out from ministry experience, ideas that affect input and become new, more relevant input for the learner. (Clinton & Clinton 1991:1-16)

Early Ministry Assignment P (MASG): Describes a ministry experience which is more permanent than a ministry task, yet has the same basic pattern of entry, ministry, closure, and transition out of the ministry situation and through which God gives new insights to the leader so as to expand influence capacity and responsibility toward future leadership. (Clinton 1989:200)

Effective Methodology: Is some ministry insight around which the leader can pass on to others the essentials of doing something or using something or being something, that is, a means of effectively delivering some important ministry of that leader which enhances life purpose or moves toward ultimate contribution. (Clinton 1995b:39)

Focal Value: Is a dominant controlling perspective (a leadership value) which interweaves itself throughout a person's ministry and usually can be traced to a critical incident. (Clinton 1995b:19)

Historical Mentor: Refers to a person now dead whose life or ministry, at least in part, is written in a biographical or autobiographical form, and is used as an example to indirectly impart skills, lessons of life and ministry, and values which empower another person. (Clinton & Clinton 1991:10-5)

Indirect Influence: This is not bound by time meaning that influence is exerted in the absence of the one exerting the influence. This is done primarily through other mediums such as printed (books), electronic or any other means. (Clinton 1988:228)

Life Purpose: Is a burden-like calling, a task or driving force or achievement, which motivates a leader to fulfill something or to see something done. (Clinton 1995b:35)

Like Attracts like M.2: It describes as early gift recognition pattern frequently seen in potential leaders in which those potential leaders are intuitively attracted to leaders who have like spiritual gifts. (Clinton 1989:360)

Literary Processing Item P (LI): Refers to the means whereby God is able to teach leaders lessons for their own lives through the writings of others. (Clinton 1995a:184)

Ministry Insights: God will give ministry breakthroughs, insights that help us to minister effectively. Many times this will necessitate a paradigm shift with regard to our ministry means. In any case, a number of these ministry insights will be seen repeated throughout our life time as we become more focused about our life purpose. (Clinton 1995b:51)

Ministry Affirmation Process Item P (MAF):	Is a special kind of destiny experience in which God gives approval to a leader in terms of some ministry assignment in particular or some ministry experience in general which results in a renewed sense of purpose for the leader. (Clinton 1989:267)
Ministry Conflict P (CONF):	Shaping activities of God which utilize adverse reactions in a given ministry situation to teach a leader valuable lessons. (Clinton 1995a:492)
Negative Processing Item P (NEG):	It refers to the special processing which involves God's use of events, people, conflict, persecution, or experiences, all focusing on the negative, so as to free up a person from the situation in order to enter the next phase of development with a new abandonment and revitalized interest. (Clinton 1995a:255)
Organizational Influence:	Is that domain of sphere of influence which indicates a measure of people being influenced by a person in organizational leadership via indirect, direct, and organizational power. (Clinton 1989:228)
Paradigm Shift P (PS):	Refers to God's use of an incident or series of incidents to impress upon the leader a major new perspective for use in ministry. (Clinton 1995a:190)
Sphere of Influence:	Refers to the totality of people being influenced and for whom a leader will give an account to God. (Clinton 1995a:227)
Spiritual Authority:	A term in leadership development theory referring to a source of credibility from God that permits leaders to influence followers. More technically, that characteristic of a God-anointed leader developed upon an experiential power base that enables him to influence followers through persuasion, force of modeling, and moral expertise. (Clinton 1988:255) Spiritual authority is not a goal but rather a byproduct. (Clinton 1988:155).
Spiritual Formation:	Refers to the development of the inner-life of the person of God so that, the person experiences more of the life of Christ, reflects more Christ-like characteristics in personality and in everyday relationship, and increasingly knows the power and presence of Christ in ministry. (Clinton 1989:72)
Spiritual Warfare Process Item P (SW):	Refers to those instances in ministry where the leader discerns that ministry conflict is primarily supernatural in its source and essence and resorts to various power items to solve the problem in such a way that leadership capacities, notably spiritual authority, is expanded. (Clinton 1989:238)
Starting-Point-Plus Process:	God begins where people are at and progressively reveals Himself and applicable truth to move them toward supracultural ideas. (Clinton 1995c:2)
Time-line:	Is the linear display along a horizontal axis which is broken up into development phases. (Clinton 1989:293)
Unique Time-line:	Refers to a time-line describing a given leader's lifetime which will have unique development PHASES bearing labels expressing that uniqueness. (Clinton 1989:294)
Word Process Item P (WI):	Is an instance in which a leader receives a word from God which significantly affects a leader's guidance, committal, decision making, personal value system, spiritual formation, spiritual authority, or ministry philosophy. (Clinton 1989a:182)

APPENDIX C: Focal Findings

The findings presented here, are from the conclusion of Dr. Clinton's **Focused Lives** along with insights comparing the life of Shirley Raper with the eight leaders studied by Clinton. Shirley Raper left behind quite a legacy.
Ultimate Contribution Sets Compared (Clinton 1995a:450)

Key:
x = some
xx = definite yes
xxx= very much so

Person	Saint	SP	Mentor	Fam	PR	Pioneer	Change Person	Founder.	Artist	Stab.	Rschr.	Wrtr.	Prom
Simeon			xxx		x								xxx
Gordon	xx	xxx	x		xxx	x	xxx	x	x	xx	x	x	xxx
Brengle	xxx		xx		xxx							xx	xxx
Morgan		xx			xxx					x		xxx	xxx
Jaffray					xxx	xx		xxx		xx	xxx	xx	xxx
McQuilkin	xxx		x		xxx			x		xxx		xx	xxx
Mears			xxx		xx	x		xxx				xx	xxx
Maxwell					xxx			xx				xx	xxx
Shirley Raper	xxx		xxx	xx				xx					xx

Definitions

Ultimate Contribution: A **legacy** that a leader will leave behind after life is over. Leaders usually have several of these.

Saint: A model life, not a perfect one, but a life that others want to emulate.

Stylistic Practitioner: It is a model ministry style, which sets the pace for others and which other ministries seek to emulate.

Family: Promotes a God-fearing family, leaving behind children who walk with God carrying on that Godly heritage.

Mentor: A productive ministry with individuals, small groups, etc.

Public Rhetorician: A productive public ministry with large groups.

Pioneer: A person who starts apostolic ministries.

Change Person: A person who rights wrongs and injustices in society, churches, and mission organizations.

Artist: A person who has creative breakthroughs in life and ministry and introduces innovation.

Founder: A person who starts a new organization to meet a need or capture the essence of some movement or the like.

Stabilizer:	It is a person, who can help a fledgling organization develop or can help an older organization move toward efficiency and effectiveness. In other words, help solidify an organization.
Researcher:	Develops new ideation by studying various things.
Writer:	Captures new ideas and reproduces them in written format to help and inform others.
Promoter:	Effectively distributes new ideas and/or other ministry related things.

APPENDIX D: Finishing Well Characteristics

Comparative Listing of Finishing Well Characteristics

Six Characteristic of Finishing Well (Clinton 1995a:455)

1. Maintain a personal vibrant relationship with God right up to the end.
2. Maintain a learning posture and learn from various kinds of sources – life especially.
3. They portray Christ-likeness in character as evidenced by the fruit of the Spirit in their lives.
4. They know how to apply truth to their lives.
5. Leaders who leave behind one or more ultimate contributions.
6. They walk with a growing awareness of a sense of destiny and see some or all of it fulfilled.

Nine Leaders and the Six Characteristics
Key:
The leaders listed are taken from Dr. Clinton's **Focused Lives** book. Shirley Raper is also included. The number in the chart corresponds to the number by the finishing well characteristic listed above.
x= some
xx= a definite yes
xxx= very much so

Leader	No. 1	No. 2	No. 3	No. 4	No. 5	No. 6
Simeon	xx	xx	xxx	x	xxx	x
Gordon	xx	xxx	xxx	xx	xxx	x
Brengle	xxx	xxx	xxx	xxx	xxx	xxx
Morgan	xx	xxx	xxx	xxx	xxx	xx
Jaffray	xxx	xxx	xxx	xxx	xxx	xxx
McQuilkin	xxx	xxx	xxx	xx	xxx	xxx
Mears	xxx	xxx	xxx	xxx	xxx	x
Maxwell	xx	xx	xxx	xx	xxx	xx
Shirley Raper	xxx	xxx	xxx	xxx	xx	xx

APPENDIX E: Destiny Log

Shirley did not live with a cognitive sense of destiny. Her radical committal to the Lord is what shaped her destiny, "I am going to find out what this man wants and I am going to do it."[70] As one traces her life, her destiny revelation,[71] preparation,[72] and fulfillment[73] become evident. Even though she was not destiny-minded, one of her favorite sayings, "I'll see you in the plan" subtly captures the essence of destiny. The following chart tracks her destiny fulfillment. The chart lists in progression her destiny preparation, revelation, and fulfillment. Some of her destiny experiences are specific to a particular thread, others are not. That is reflected in this destiny log.

This destiny log is different from the destiny processing and type listed on page 50. The purpose of this destiny log is to track the different major roles and how they developed over her life. There are four destiny threads: the Military Thread, the Mother of Israel Thread, the Leadership Thread, and the Celebration Thread. Each one is distinct yet they are all intertwined.

Progression	Destiny Label **Military Thread**	Description **Shirley is called to pray for the military.**
Preparation	God, are you there?	As a child she would stare into the night sky and ask God if he was real, while at the same time praying to him with specific requests. This happened against a backdrop of her mother and aunts' involvement in occultic practices and the absence of Christian training. This preparation hinted at a future life of intercession.
Preparation	Patriotic Songs	As a child patriotic songs always caused an emotional response of tears whenever Shirley heard the music. This emotional response to patriotic and military theme songs hinted at a future calling upon her life of praying for the military.
Preparation	Scrapbook	During WWII Shirley kept a scrapbook of newspaper clippings of AP war stories. This was another confirmation of how God wired her to have a heart for the military.
Revelation	POW Bracelet	During the Vietnam War Shirley was given the POW Bracelet of a Navy pilot shot down in North Vietnam. She prayed for him everyday while he remained a POW during the war. He lived through captivity.
Revelation	Front Porch Radio Program	In the late 1980's Shirley co-hosted a monthly radio program. A young Army Lieutenant listened. Afterwards he requested to meet Shirley. She is a divine contact and in time became a spiritual mother to him.
Revelation	Revelation Label:	Some time after the Vietnam War ended, Shirley had a dream about

[70] Shirley made that comment on the night she accepted the Lord.

[71] Destiny revelation "is a shaping process used by God in which He reveals something of His purposes for a leader in such a way as to inspire that leader to go on and serve God knowing that God's hand is on his/her life." (Clinton 1995a:487) According to this definition, Shirley was very much aware of her destiny revelation although she would not have used that term. What she did understand and recognize was God's hand upon her life shaping her character through the process items she experienced.

[72] Destiny preparation is the "shaping processes used by God in the earliest stages of a leader's initial awareness of a sense of destiny which hints at destiny." (Clinton 1995a:487) It is evident that God began destiny preparation in Shirley's life while she was a child in the absence of a godly heritage.

[73] Destiny fulfillment refers to the "shaping processes used by God in the latter stages of a leader's life in which the leader sees a sense of destiny coming to pass." (Clinton 1995a:487) This is beginning to happen for Shirley. Her religious order is structured to continue on after her death with future leadership already set in place.

	"Abandoned"	prisoners in cages with men guarding them with rifles. She had the same dream two nights in a row. Eerily she could not shake the feeling of absolute abandonment which enveloped her. She shared the dream with a friend who was in the military and he told her that what she saw was a POW camp in North Vietnam. This dream, in the early 1980's was her call to being praying for the POW/MIA's abandoned by the United States after the Vietnam War.
Fulfillment	High Ranking Officer	The young Lieutenant is now a General. Mother Shirley prays for him. She also prays for other high ranking officers.
Fulfillment	Father/Son	Shirley meets the son of the POW Navy pilot whose bracelet she wore during the Vietnam War. He is a high ranking Navy officer. In time, he becomes a spiritual son.
Fulfillment	Will you pray for me?	At a military gathering to honor the wounded, a General observed people approaching Mother Shirley without solicitation for hugs. The observant General asked to meet Mother Shirley. The General then asked if Mother Shirley would be willing to pray for her.
	Mother of Israel Thread	**Shirley is called to be a spiritual mother to hundreds and thousands.**
Preparation	God, are you there?	As a child she would stare into the night sky and ask God if he was real while at the same time praying to him with specific requests. This happened against a backdrop of her mother and aunts' involvement in occultic practices and the absence of Christian training. This preparation hinted at a future life of intercession.
Preparation	The Candy Bar	As a child, Shirley had to sleep in the living room of her aunt and uncle after her parent's divorce. During that time her mother suffered an emotional breakdown. Her relatives did not want Shirley. In the evening they would eat candy and drink soda in front of her as her bed was in the living room. This incident forged the value that she would always share. It made her a compassionate mother later in life.
Preparation	Pop Tyndale	He was a neighbor who was the father of a daughter Shirley's age. Shirley was invited to attend a southern baptist church with him and his daughter. Shirley always felt that he must have prayed for her. From this incident, it appears that God will send non-family members to pray for the spiritual development of an individual if there are no family members to bequeath a spiritual heritage through modeling and prayer. Even though Shirley's grandmother read the Bible to her on a few occasions, it is not known if her grandmother prayed for her grand-daughter. There is no mention of attending church. Her mother and aunts sought guidance through occultic practices.
Revelation	Mother of Israel	Shirley received a prophetic word from Robert McMillan that someday she would be a Mother of Israel.
Fulfillment	The Mother Habit	She begins to wear a gray nun-like habit. People start calling her "Mother Shirley."
Fulfillment	"Amma"	The Syrian Orthodox priests all address her as "amma," meaning mother in Greek. It is a term of honor.
Fulfillment	Spiritual Mother	She has spiritual children in many states. They always come to see her, some driving great distances to spend a few days to be in her presence.
	Leadership Thread:	**God called Shirley to be a leader of both men and women teaching and modeling the manifest and unbiased love of Christ so that healing can happen.**
Preparation	God, are you there?	As a child she would stare into the night sky and ask God if he was real while at the same time praying to him with specific requests. This happened against a backdrop of her mother and aunts' involvement in occultic practices and the absence of Christian

		training. This preparation hinted at a future life of intercession.
Preparation	Will You Teach the Elders	This was a leadership affirmation hinting at her future role in teaching the leaders within the church. She turned the pastor down as she was a new Christian.
Preparation	Substitute Pastor	Shirley was asked by numerous pastors to fill in for them when they were sick or away on vacation at a time when women did not preach.
Revelation	Church Beyond the Walls	God called Shirley to lead those beyond the walls of the Church, meaning the universal Church.
Fulfillment	Chapel	Mother Shirley will be ordained as a Syrian Orthodox Priest in the fall of 2008. She currently pastors the church that meets in the chapel next to their home.
	Celebration Thread	**God called Mother Shirley to teach and model to others how to celebrate the majesty and splendor of God through worship.**
Revelation	The Football Game	In 1969, Shirley watched a football game with her children. Taken by the energy people put into the half-time show to celebrate football, she felt that Christians should celebrate Christ with the same passion and energy.
Preparation	Dance Teams	Shirley formed dance, flag, tambourine, and sword teams to perform in processionals to celebrate the presence of God.
Fulfillment	Spiritual Retreats	She hosts spiritual retreats in which the focus is to celebrate the presence of the Lord through extended worship. Teaching is minimal.

APPENDIX F: Personal Life Mandate

My Life Purpose:

My life purpose is primarily to be a mother in Israel who expresses both the manifest and unbiased love of Christ to all. I am called to be a bridge to young adults, loving a generation that grew up as emotional orphans, ministering to and loving them as a mother would her children through a one-on-one setting or in group settings. I am called by God to be a spiritual mother to leaders of leaders, especially military leaders, to pray for them and to encourage them. Secondarily, I am called to the priesthood as a pastor-leader of the flock God sends to me.

My Effective Methodologies:

My effective and unique methodologies revolve around my natural talents and how I am spiritually gifted. I love people. I practice a form of evangelism called "as you go evangelism" meaning that I frequent the same businesses and as I love people with the manifest and unbiased love of Christ, they respond. My evangelistic method is to love people where they are at and not to judge them. God does the rest from salvation to profound spiritual and physical healing in their lives.

Specifically my effective methodologies center on the ability to mentor one-on-one, in small groups or in mid-sized groups. The mentoring happens informally through lunches, bible studies, hospitality with people traveling great distances to spend time with me in my home, non-formally through spiritual retreats, or through the sister/brotherhood. Story telling makes my mentoring powerful. I am a master story-teller using the stories from my life to illustrate principles from God's word. I constantly study God's word so that my teaching is grounded in Truth. I pray everyday for my physical and spiritual children. I use the discipline of celebrating the majesty and splendor of God through dance and worship. Generosity expressed through the giving of gifts, be they spiritual or temporal is another methodology.

My Major Role:

I understand that in order to fulfill my life purpose I need to play a foundational key role as a mother, an intercessor, a teacher, mentor, and leader, which I have done. While my dominate role is that of a spiritual mother to those God brings to me, I under gird that with intercession. I am called to pray for my physical and spiritual children. I am also called to teach, whether that is a bible study, church, iconography, or cooking. I am a leader-pastor of the church God gathers in my chapel. I am the leader of a religious order. As I transition into afterglow, the roles of teacher, leader, and mentor may decrease due to my age, but my role of mother and intercessor will remain constant.

Ultimate Contribution:

I know that if I am to leave behind a lasting legacy of motherhood I must invest in my spiritual children so that they will mature into Christ-centered spiritual fathers and mothers, nurturing the next generation of emotional orphans. I will do this by modeling the manifest and unbiased love of Christ so my natural and spiritual children can see it in action. Through multiple trials, persecutions, and losses covered by the grace and love of Christ I learned how to walk as a **saint** because I was willing to pay the cost of following Jesus. I will **mentor** the emotional orphans that come to me seeking a spiritual mother. I will spend time with them imparting spiritual values that they in turn will be able to impart to the generation after them. I will pray for and mentor the military leaders God sends my way. I used my organizational skills, leadership skills, and the skills of a **founder** to establish a religious order. I structured The Order of the Myrrhbearers to continue on after my death so that my legacy will continue to bless others with the manifest and unbiased love of Christ. My humor, organizational skills, discernment, and leadership skills all provide the infrastructure for my role as a **promoter**. Years ago, God gave me a revelation about the importance of celebrating His majesty and splendor with pageantry. I effectively distributed these new ideas to others by forming dance teams, flag teams, and tambourine teams into processionals in order to honor God as the King of the universe. My greatest legacy is my **family**. The manifest and unbiased love of Christ is the common denominator linking each of these ultimate contributions together.

BIBLIOGRAPHY

Clinton, J. Robert.

1988 **The Making of a Leader**. Colorado Springs: NavPress.

1989a **Leadership Emergence Theory.** Altadena: Barnabas Publishers.

1995a **Focused Lives: Inspirational Life Changing Lessons from Eight Leaders Who Finished Well**. Altadena, CA: Barnabas Publishers.

1995b **Strategic Concepts That Clarify A Focused Life.** Altadena, CA: Barnabas Publishers.

1995c Article: *Gender and Leadership: My Personal Pilgrimage.* Altadena, CA: Barnabas Publishers.

1997 **Having a Ministry That Lasts: Becoming a Bible Centered Leader.** Altadena, CA: Barnabas Publishers.

Clinton, J. Robert & Clinton, Richard W.

1991 **Mentor Handbook: Detailed Guidelines and Helps for Christian Mentors and Mentorees**. Altadena, CA: Barnabas Publishers.

Grudem, Wayne A.

1996 General Editor: **Are Miraculous Gifts for Today?** Grand Rapids, MI: Zondervan Publishing House.

Raper, Shirley

2006 Taped personal interviews in Sparta, Tennessee.
2008

Upham, T. C.

1984 **The Life of Jeanne Guyon: The Life of the Most Influential Woman in Christian History**. Jacksonville, FL: SeedSowers Publishing House.

Notes:

Notes:

Notes:

Notes:

Notes:

Notes:

Notes:

Notes:

Notes:

Notes:

Shirley Raper
She persistently pursued God in all she did.
No cost was too great in following Jesus.

www.ingramcontent.com/pod-product-compliance
Lightning Source LLC
LaVergne TN
LVHW080923110826
845155LV00039B/197

* 9 7 8 1 9 3 2 8 1 4 0 1 9 *